The Ultimate

ROAD TRIP
ACTIVITY
BOOK

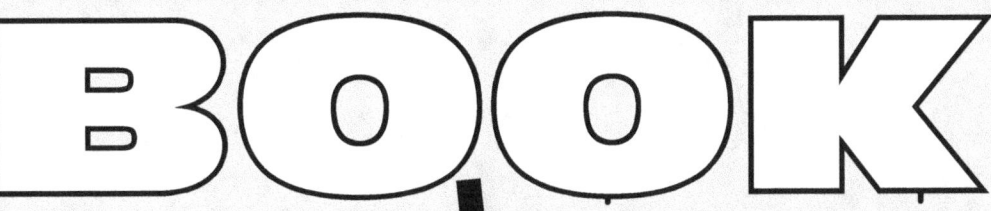

for **Kids**

Connor Williams

ISBN: 978-1-64845-105-8

Copyright @ 2023 by LAK Publishing

All rights reserved. No part of this book may be reproduced, scanned, or distributed in any printed or electronic form without permission. Please do not participate in or encourage piracy of copyrighted materials in violation of the author's rights. Purchase only authorized editions.

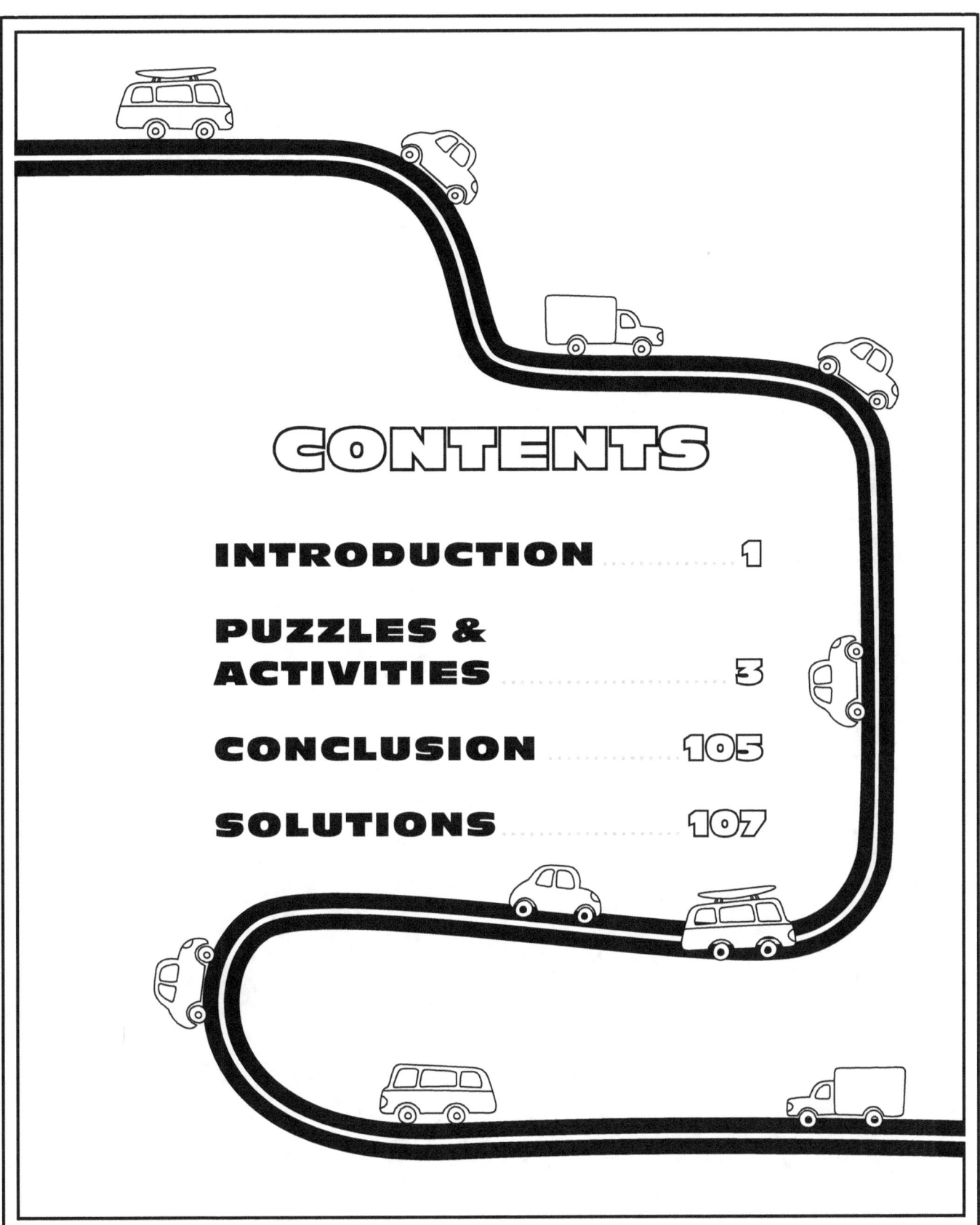

CONTENTS

INTRODUCTION 1

PUZZLES & ACTIVITIES 3

CONCLUSION 105

SOLUTIONS 107

INTRODUCTION

COLOR THESE IN ON EVERY PAGE!

Who doesn't love a road trip? But let's be honest—as fun and as exciting as a road trip is, traveling a long distance by car is nothing of the sort…

Getting to your destination is brilliant. But the hour after hour of driving that comes before then—just sat in the back of the car, as mile after mile of roads go by!—can make road trips very boring. Not to worry, though, because that's precisely what this book is here to fix!

This is your very own **Road Trip Activity Book**, specially designed to make traveling fun, and pass your time in the back of the car as quickly as possible. Here you'll find 100 picture and number puzzles, mazes, word games, and letter jumbles, perfect for keeping your brain engaged and the minutes ticking by.

So let's get started! Turn the page to take on your very first brainteaser…

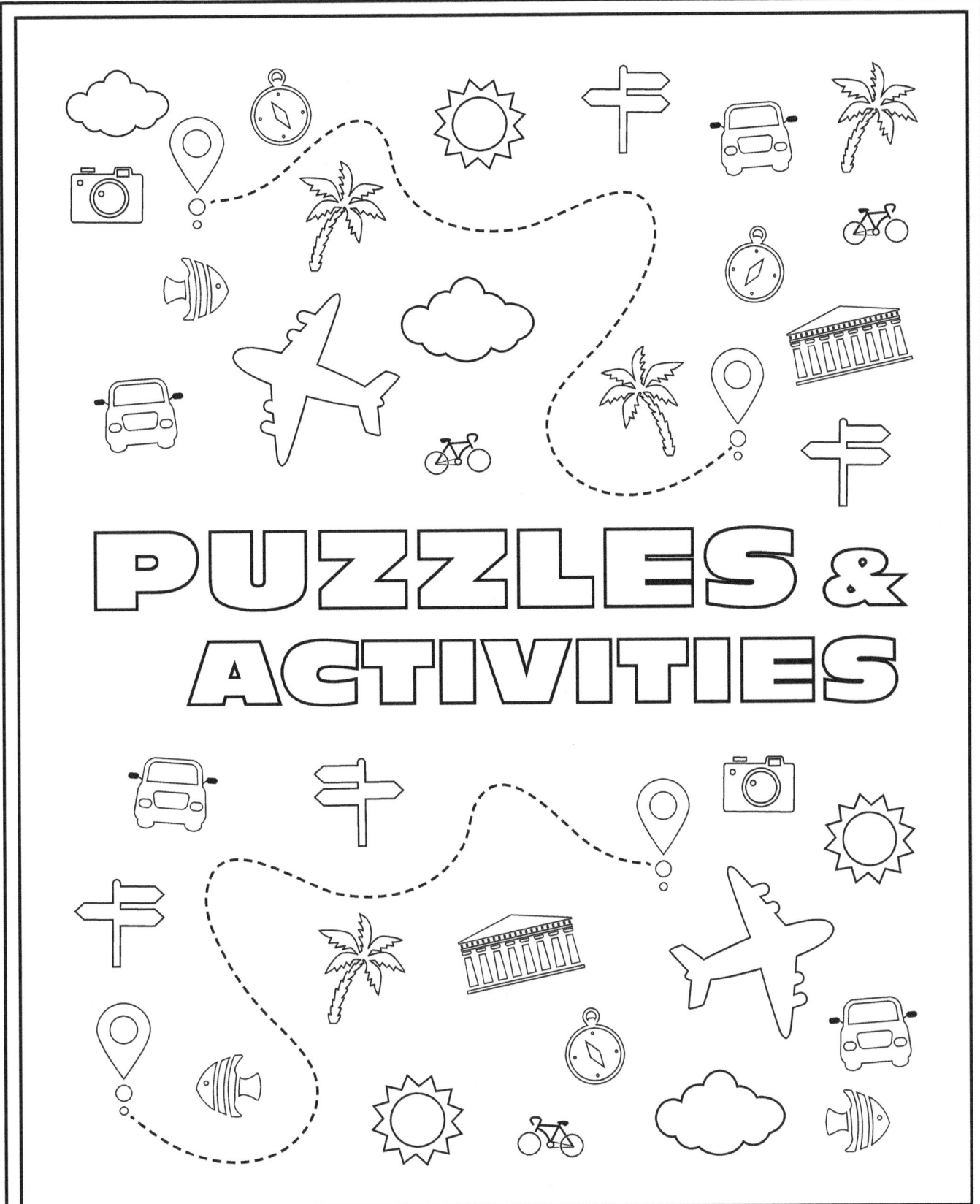

Let's start where all good road trips start—by getting in the car! Can you find these 10 vehicle parts hidden in the grid below?

- [ ] **DASHBOARD**
- [ ] **EXHAUST**
- [ ] **GLOVEBOX**
- [ ] **HOOD**
- [ ] **LIGHTS**
- [ ] **MIRRORS**
- [ ] **SEATBELT**
- [ ] **SPARE / TIRE**
- [ ] **TRUNK**
- [ ] **WINDOW**

```
T  R  U  N  K  H  G  E  A  J
D  N  B  N  E  O  U  U  D  S
Q  R  U  E  N  O  V  R  E  R
W  L  A  E  X  D  C  A  R  O
T  I  W  O  E  H  T  Y  A  R
G  G  N  A  B  B  A  E  P  R
J  H  U  D  E  H  R  U  S  I
F  T  M  L  O  I  S  E  S  M
F  S  T  N  T  W  T  A  I  T
X  O  B  E  V  O  L  G  D  U
```

Take the car to the mountains!

Which of these road signs appears the most times in the grid below?

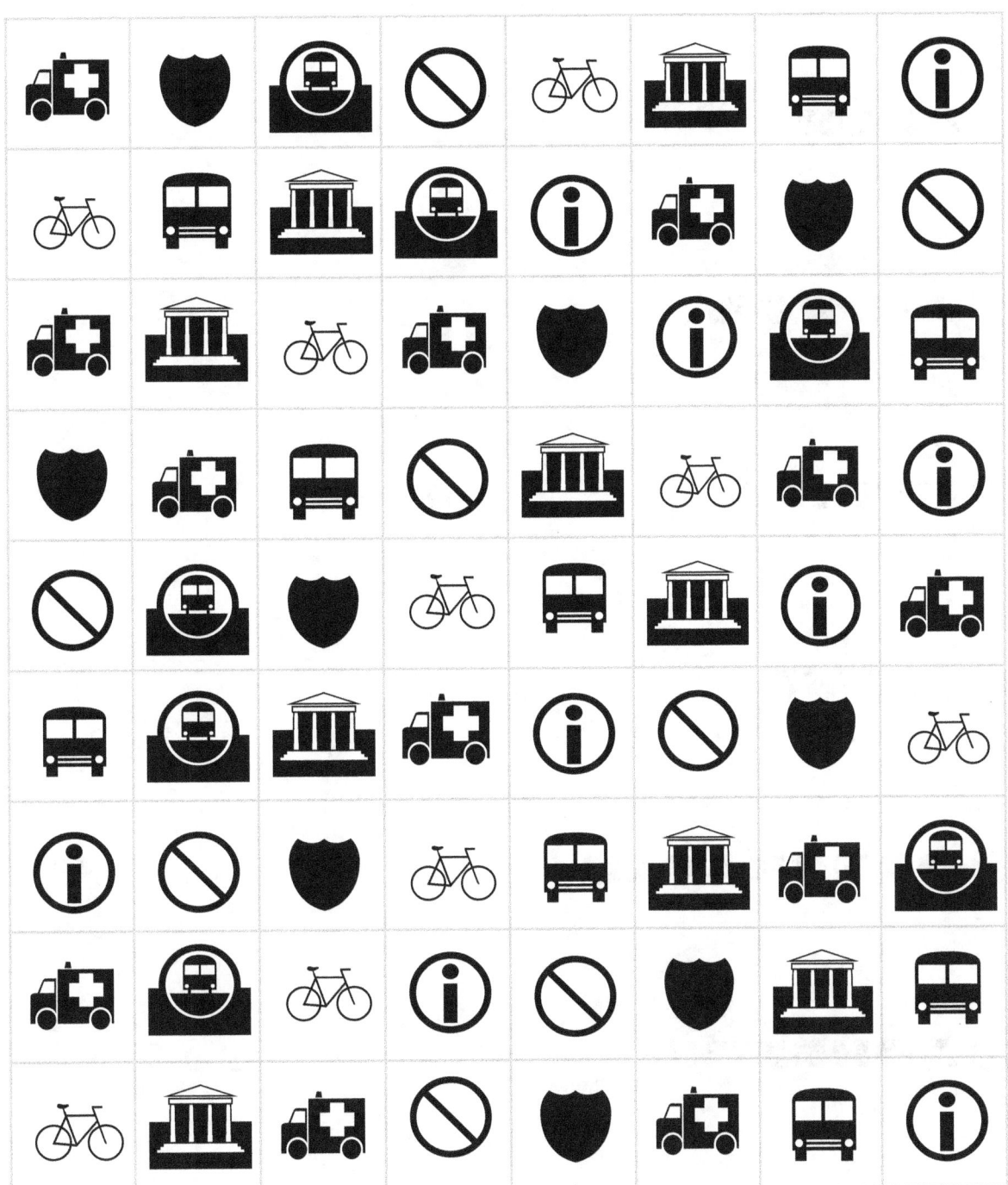

Six things you might be able to see right now inside a car have been jumbled up here. Can you unjumble them?

1 DAORI _ _ D _ _

2 DINWOW _ I _ _ _ _

3 VIRRED _ R _ _ _ R

4 LAPED P _ _ _ _

5 DANHKAREB H _ _ _ B _ _ K

6 ADHESTER HE _ _ _ E _ T

Before you go on a long trip, of course, you need to pack your bag! Take a look at the list below and draw each item in the suitcase.

☐ **CAMERA** ☐ **BOOK** ☐ **PEN** ☐ **DRINK** ☐ **CHARGER**

Time for a match up! Can you correctly match the road sign on the left to its pair on the right? The first one has been done for you to make a start.

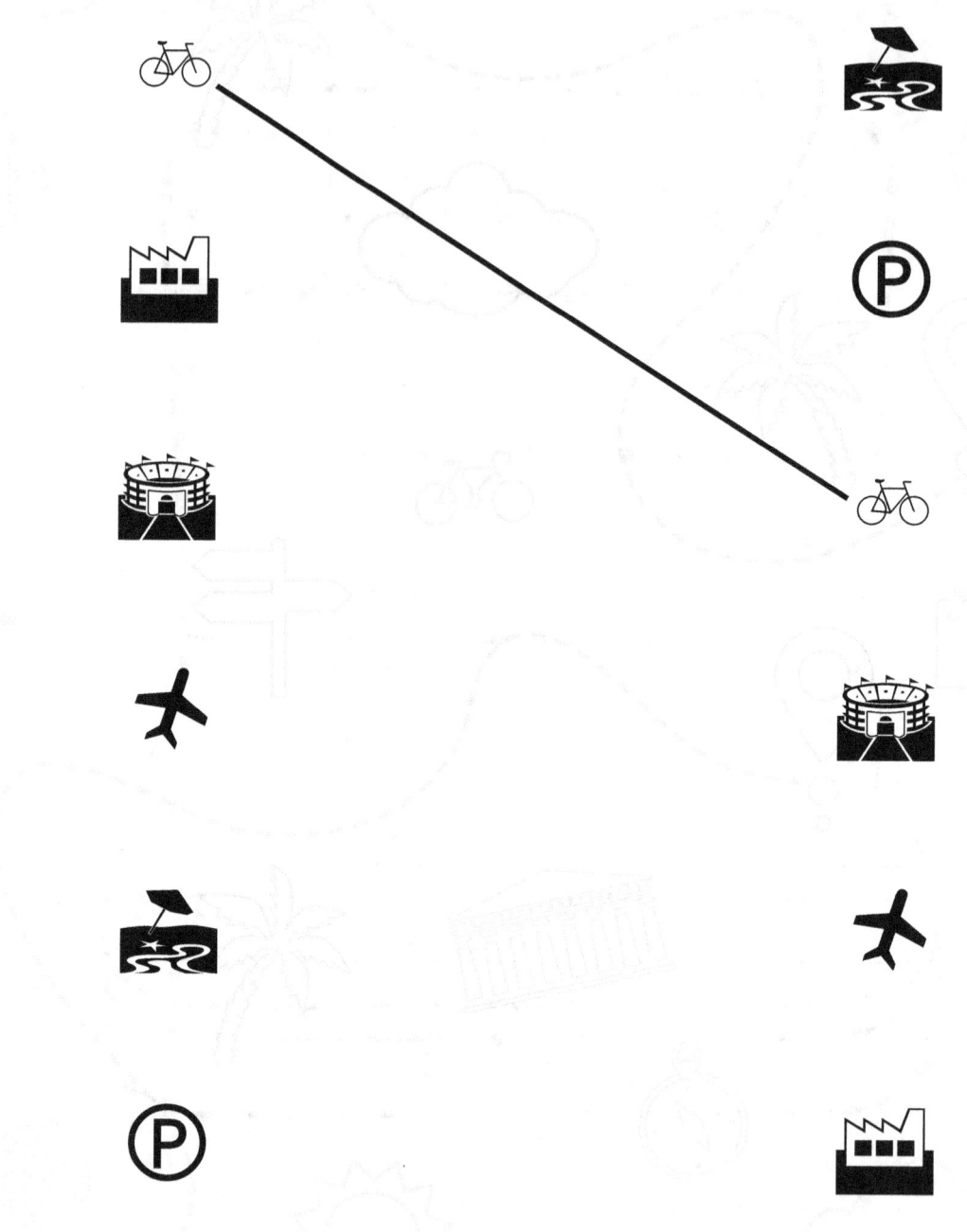

Let's head to the airport this time! Can you find your way there?

The words below all connect together in the grid. Can you figure out which word goes where?

- ALLEY
- AVENUE
- BLOCK
- DEAD END
- HIGHWAY
- INTERSECTION
- RIGHT TURN
- ROAD
- STREET

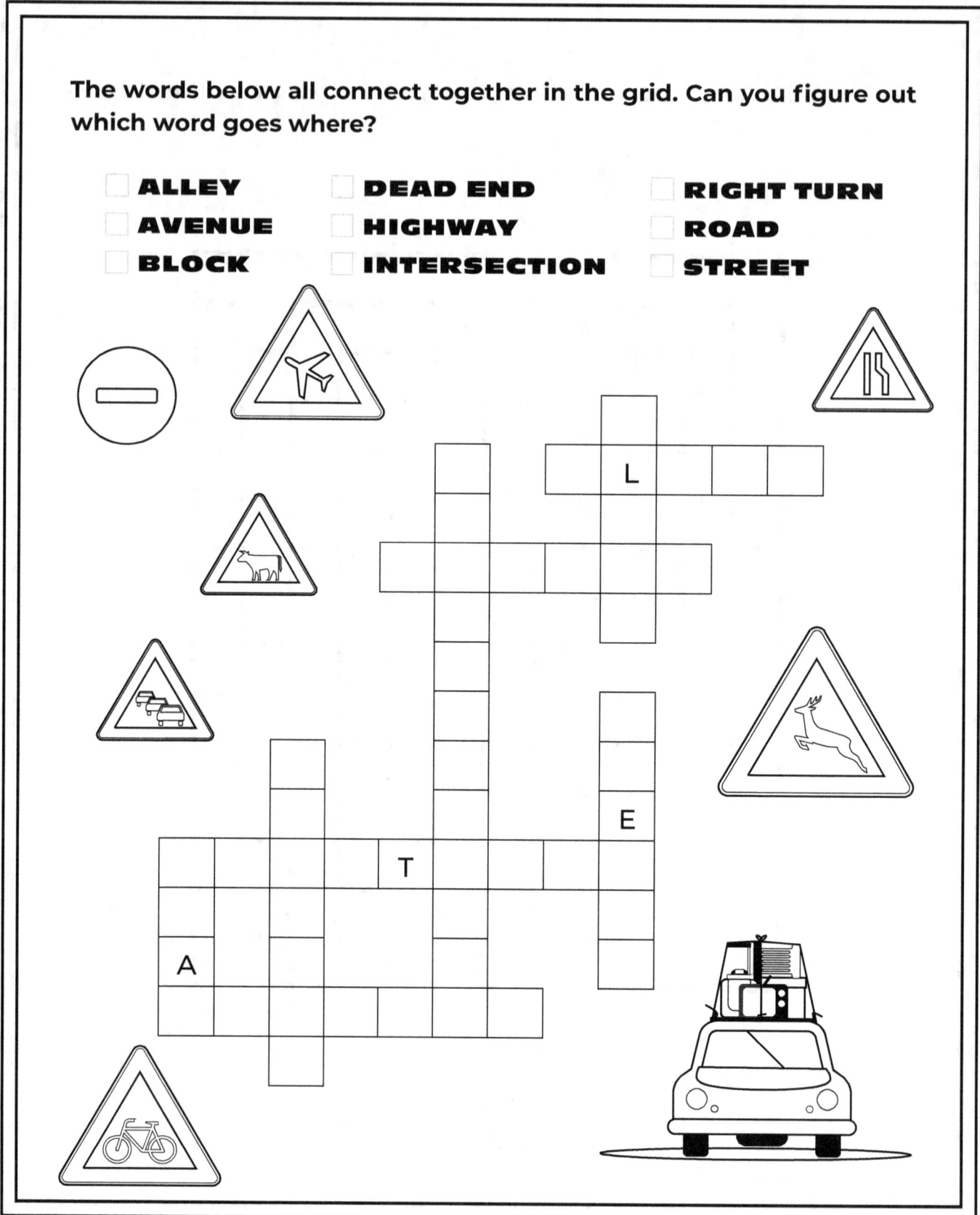

There are lots more vehicles on the road besides yours! Can you unscramble their names below?

① **RUCKT**   _ _ R _ _

② **PEEJ**   J _ _ _

③ **AXIT**   _ _ _ I

④ **PKCUPI**   _ _ _ K _ P

⑤ **OTMIROBKE**   M _ _ _ R _ _ K _

⑥ **MBACLUANE**   _ M _ _ L _ _ E

Are there more left turns or right turns on this page?

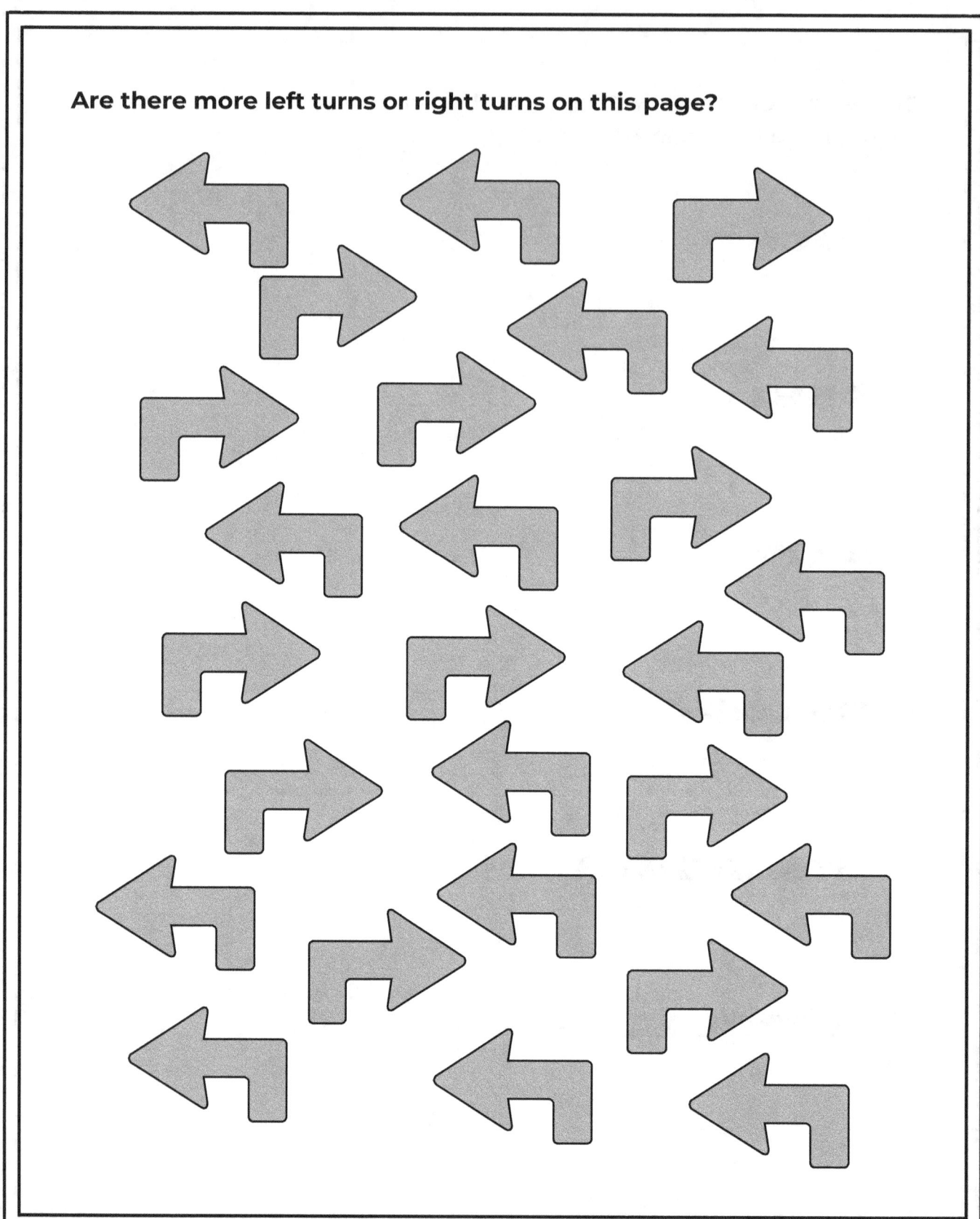

We've arrived at the airport! How many of these air travel words can you find in the grid below?

- ☐ **AIRPLANE**
- ☐ **BAGS**
- ☐ **LUGGAGE**
- ☐ **MONEY**
- ☐ **PASSENGERS**
- ☐ **PASSPORT**
- ☐ **SUNHAT**
- ☐ **TAXI**
- ☐ **TICKETS**

```
S T S A Q B G B L T
U N R I F Y A C A U
N E E R D G E X B X
H A G P S C I N J V
A V N L C I R A O Z
T Z E A D M C P T M
P U S N C K M V Y T
X K S E G A G G U L
Q B A S T E K C I T
C U P A S S P O R T
```

Can you solve these road sum signs?

1) 50 − 30 = _____

2) 20 + 50 = _____

3) 30 ÷ 10 = _____

4) 50 + 50 = _____

The answers to all these trivia questions begin with P. When you place them in the grid, another word will appear down the shaded column in the middle. What is the secret word?

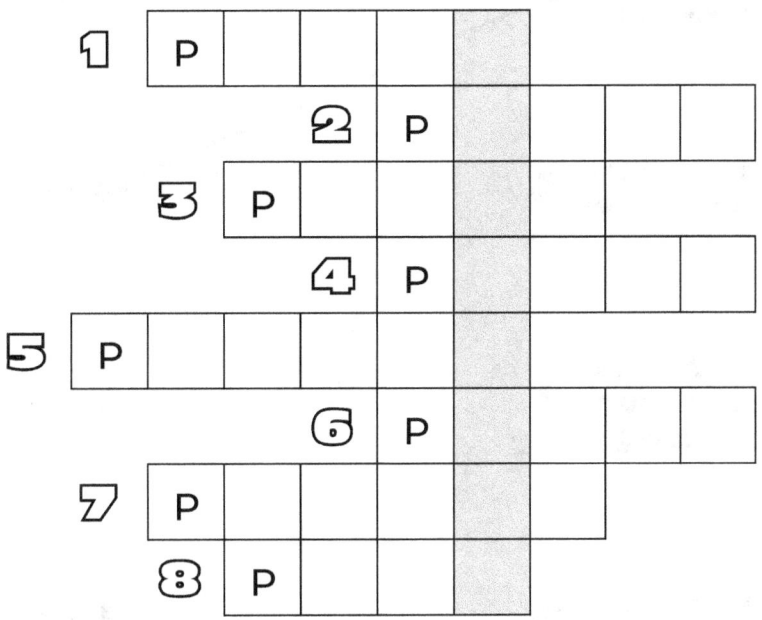

1 What's the capital city of France?

2 What musical instrument has 88 black and white keys?

3 What animal eats bamboo shoots?

4 What kind of gem does an oyster make?

5 What cushion do you rest your head on in bed?

6 What kind of food is spaghetti?

7 Indigo and violet are shades of what color?

8 What do ice hockey players hit?

Can you match the road trip word on the right with its description on the left?

- The end of your trip — DESTINATION
- It keeps you safe! — CROSSROADS
- Where you might keep your bags — RADIO
- Glass front of a vehicle — TRUNK
- It keeps you entertained with music — SEATBELT
- X-shaped road junction — WINDSHIELD

You might have seen some of these car brands on the road! Can you link them altogether in the grid below?

- ☐ CADILLAC
- ☐ LEXUS
- ☐ TOYOTA
- ☐ FERRARI
- ☐ MERCEDES
- ☐ VOLKSWAGEN
- ☐ FORD
- ☐ TESLA
- ☐ VOLVO

Let's take a trip to the zoo. Can you find your way there?

Fifteen of the letters in the grid below appear twice, while five of them only appear once. Reading from top to bottom, what do the five letters that only appear once spell out?

C	T	H	V	E	G	Y
M	O	K	B	R	P	N
A	W	B	Y	S	F	C
W	E	P	F	I	M	K
H	S	V	N	G	O	L

HIDDEN WORD: TRAIL

Take a look out of the window as you go, and you might spot some of these words that have been jumbled up! Can you unjumble them?

1 LIHSL _ _ L _ _

2 KASEL _ K _ _ _

3 FSETSRO F _ _ _ _ T _

4 ARPSK _ _ _ K _

5 MLEOTS _ O _ _ L S

6 MNTOASNIU _ _ U _ _ A _ N _

Some people travel with their luggage strapped to the roof of the car, not stored in the trunk! So pencils at the ready — draw one suitcase on the roof of the first car below, two on the roof of the second, three on the roof of the third, and four on the roof of the fourth!

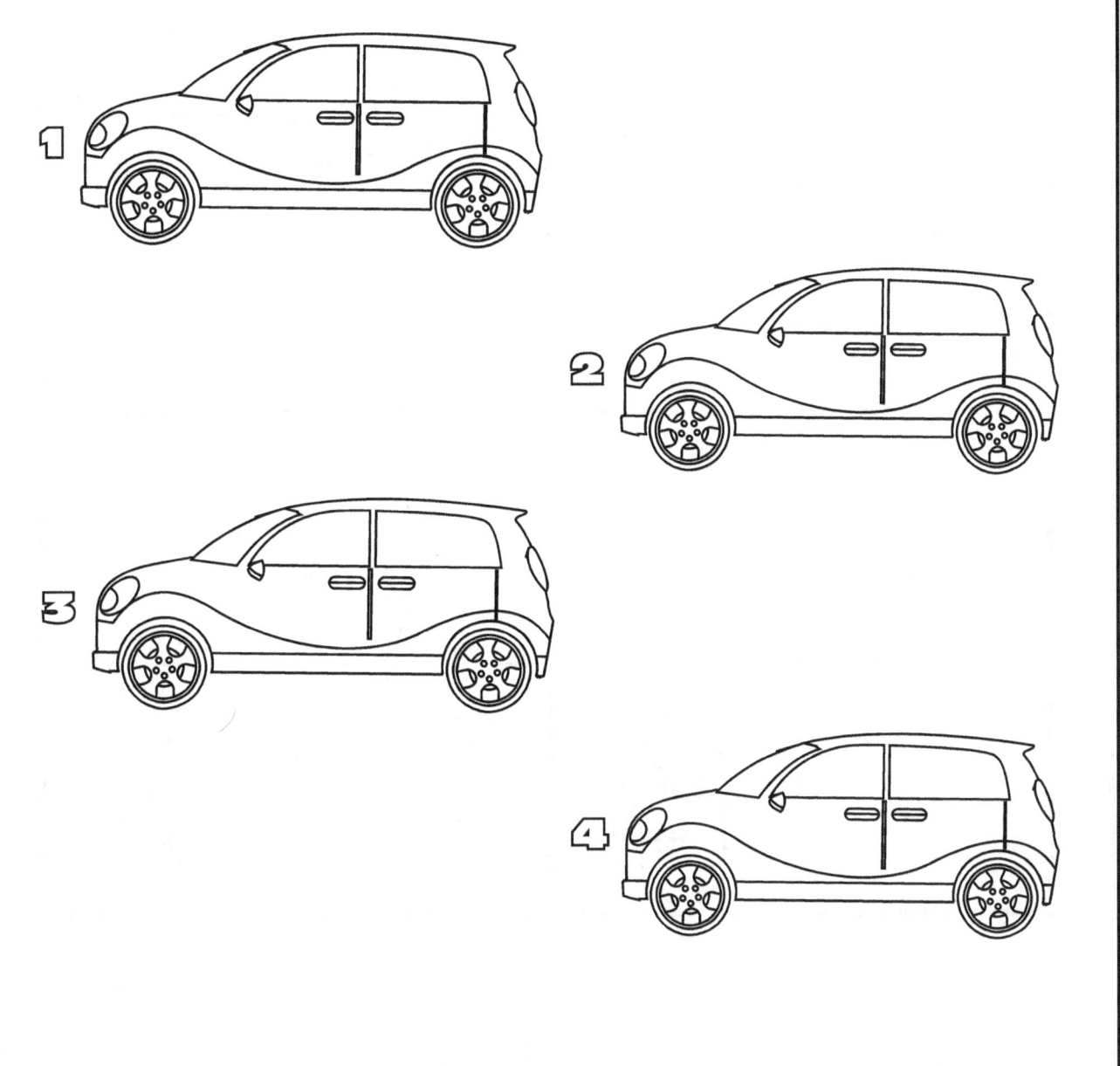

This is a picture sudoku! Can you complete the grid below so that there is just one car, one plane, one boat, and one bicycle on each row, in each column, and inside each set of four boxes? Some of the squares have been filled in for you to help you make a start!

Let's stop at the drive-thru. How many of these take out foods can you spot in the grid below?

- ☐ **BURGER**
- ☐ **CHEESE**
- ☐ **COLA**
- ☐ **FRIES**
- ☐ **HOTDOG**
- ☐ **ICECREAM**
- ☐ **LEMONADE**
- ☐ **NACHOS**
- ☐ **SAUCE**
- ☐ **WATER**

```
Y C W S T T P W N G
X H Y A Q G D W P O
S E D U W U G A S D
B E I C H A M G A T
G S I E M F T L W O
R E G R U B O E A H
R P J P F C B Q R G
L E M O N A D E T S
S O H C A N P T Z C
G N I C E C R E A M
```

Let's complete this driving scene! Can you add everything from the list below to the picture?

1. **SUN IN THE SKY**
2. **MOUNTAINS IN THE BACKGROUND**
3. **TREES BY THE ROADSIDE**
4. **BIRDS FLYING**

Let's get counting! Are there more stop signs or dead end signs on this page?

All the answers to these trivia questions begin with W. When you put their answers into the grid, another word from your road trip will appear down the shaded column in the middle. What is the secret word?

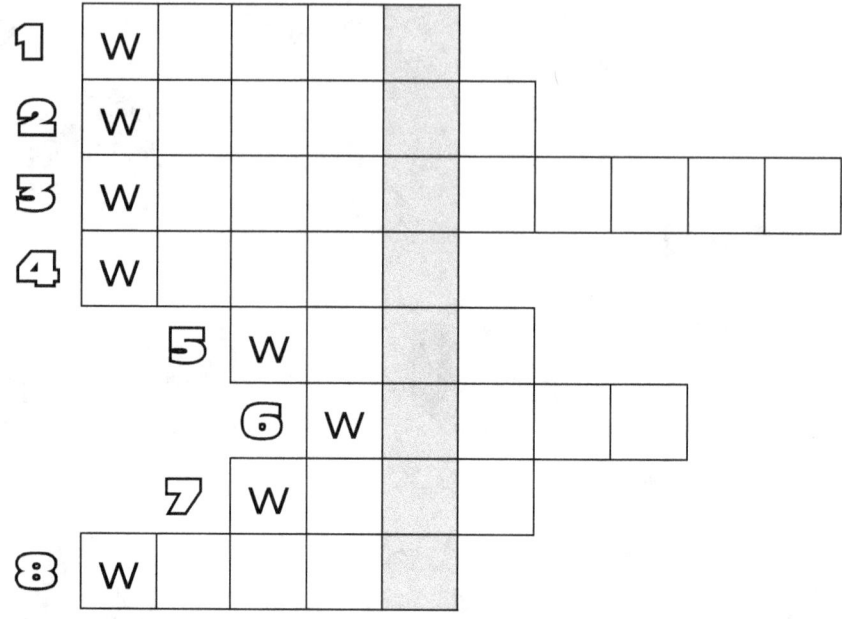

1 What are there 52 of in an entire year?

2 What animal is a tusked Arctic seal?

3 What was the surname of George, the first US president?

4 What is the joint between the arm and the hand called?

5 What is the burning string in a candle called?

6 What substance is known as H2O in science?

7 What direction lies opposite east?

8 What color is the cue ball in snooker and pool?

If you're off on holiday, some of the things you might need to take with you are jumbled up here. Can you unjumble them?

1 SNUGALSSSE _ _ N _ _ S _ S _ _

2 PSASPTRO _ _ S S _ _ _ T

3 SICUETSA _ _ _ T C _ _ E

4 HSOTRS _ _ _ _ T S

5 HTA _ _ _

6 SNUCSRNEE S _ N _ _ E E _

Who doesn't like a snack while they're driving! Can you join all these foods together in the grid below?

- ☐ BERRIES
- ☐ CANDIES
- ☐ CARROT STICKS
- ☐ CHIPS
- ☐ CHOCOLATE
- ☐ FRUITS
- ☐ NACHOS
- ☐ NUTS
- ☐ RAISINS
- ☐ TRAIL MIX

Can you solve these road sum sums?

1) 40 − 30 = _____

2) 30 + 20 = _____

3) 20 + 50 = _____

4) 40 ÷ 10 = _____

Let's stop for lunch at the café. Can you find your way there?

There are lots of buttons and lights and switches on the dashboard! How many of these can you find in the grid?

- ENGINE
- HANDBRAKE
- HEATER
- LIGHTS
- OIL
- RADIO
- WASHER
- WINDOWS

```
R A D I O L E F K E
M E K W D M R T N W
I U T Q A F Q G T I
S R L A B S I Y S N
T X M L E N H M J D
H I E Z E H D E G O
G M H K L P T N R W
I T S I K B S W E S
L P O K O R D S U I
E K A R B D N A H P
```

Fifteen of the letters in the grid below appear twice, while five of them only appear once. Reading from top to bottom, what do the five letters that only appear once spell out?

G	L	B	O	H	C	I
W	D	S	E	P	M	Q
K	A	V	P	K	D	B
Z	I	O	W	S	Q	Z
R	C	S	H	V	L	M

HIDDEN WORD: GEARS

Five friends—Amanda, Bruno, Carlo, Daniel, and Emily—each own five different modes of transport: a car, a bicycle, a boat, an airplane, and a hot air balloon. Based on the clues, can you figure out who owns what?

1. The person who owns the airplane has a name beginning with a vowel
2. The boy with the longest name owns the vehicle with the shortest name
3. The boat is not owned by girl, but the hot air balloon isn't owned by a boy
4. The truck is owned by someone with a 5-letter name
5. Carlo doesn't own anything with wheels!

AMANDA	
BRUNO	
CARLO	
DANIEL	
EMILY	

Let's get counting and drawing! Draw four passengers on board the first bus, eight passengers on the second bus, and twelve passengers on the third bus.

All the answers to these trivia questions begin with S. When you put their answers into the grid, another word from your road trip will appear down the shaded column in the middle. What is the secret word?

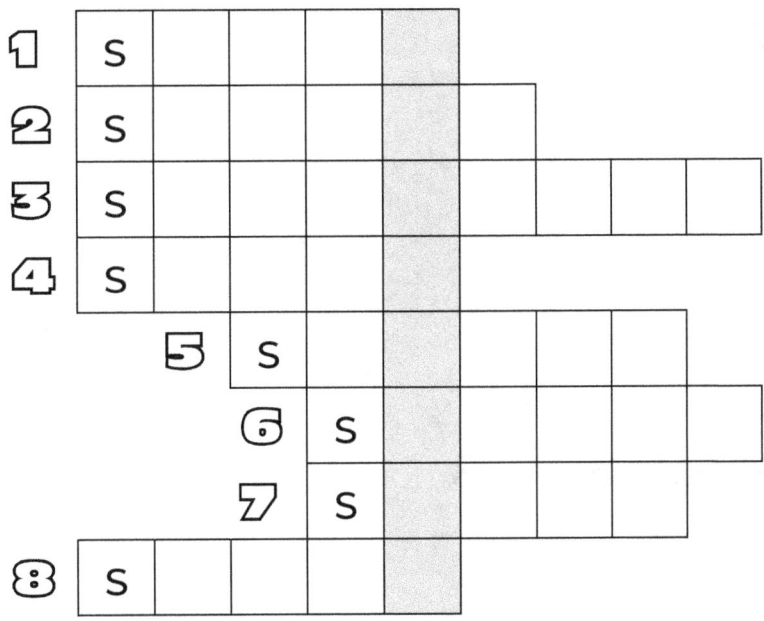

1. What kind of power is generated by the sun?

2. What kind of fish is known for swimming back upstream to breed each spring?

3. What a person's unique way of writing their own name on formal documents known as?

4. What is acoustics the science of?

5. What relation is Solange Knowles to Beyoncé?

6. What are there 50 of in the USA?

7. What single-digit number is considered lucky?

8. What are sucrose and glucose examples of?

Let's go camping! How many of these items of camping equipment can you unjumble here?

1 **NTET** _____ _____ _____

2 **GBA** _____ _____

3 **LBNAKTE** B_____ K_____

4 **TCHOR** _____ _____ H

5 **SVOTE** S_____ _____

6 **MCTHAES** M_____ H_____

Are there more ambulances or fire trucks on this page?

39

Let's head to the beach! Can you find your way there?

The words below are all things you might see while driving at night. Can you put them in the correct places in the grid, so that all the words connect together?

- FOXES
- HEADLIGHTS
- MIST
- MOON
- OWL
- PLANE
- SHOOTING STAR
- STARS
- STREETLIGHTS

The names of six car parts have been split up here, so that one half is on the left, and the other half is on the right. Can you match the two halves together correctly? The first pair has been matched already to start you off!

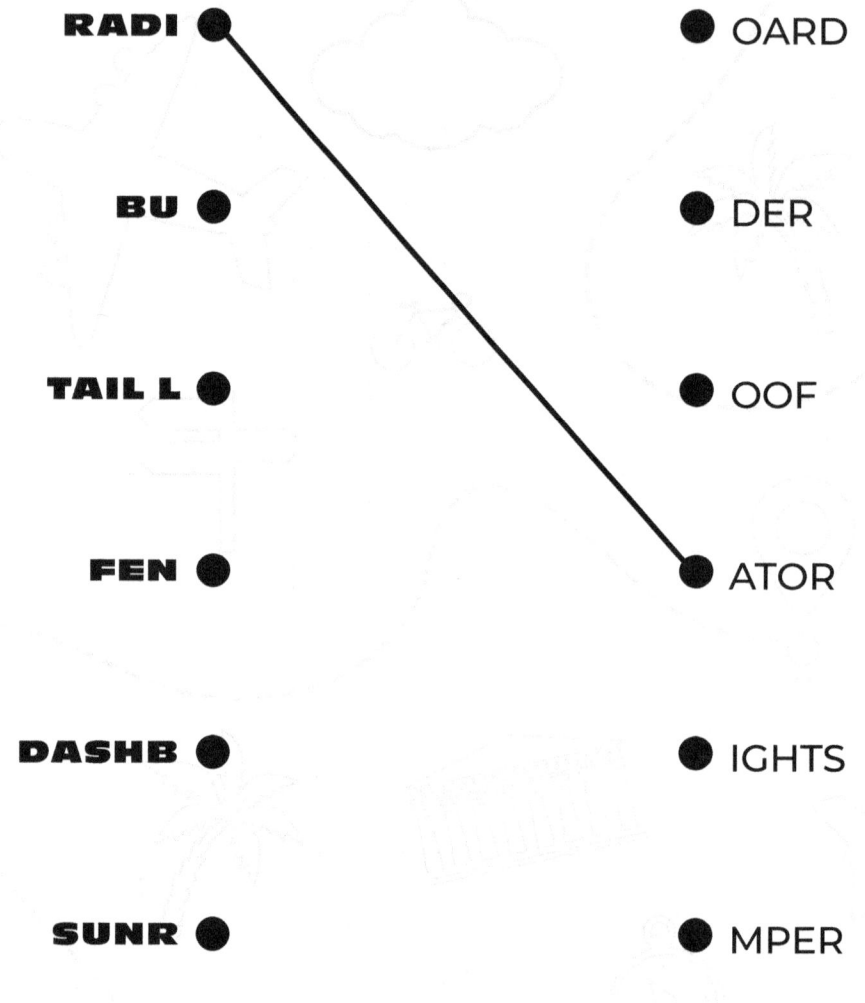

Let's flip open the glove box. How many of these items that we might find inside can you spot in the grid?

- ATLAS
- CLOTH
- GLOVES
- MANUAL
- MONEY
- NOTEPAD
- PEN
- ROADMAP
- SUNGLASSES
- TICKETS

```
R  T  L  S  B  H  C  W  Y  Y
O  I  A  E  H  G  T  M  S  P
A  C  U  S  Y  I  J  O  E  K
D  K  N  S  I  K  J  N  L  F
M  E  A  A  S  A  L  T  A  C
A  T  M  L  Y  E  N  O  M  J
P  S  Q  G  S  E  V  O  L  G
A  Z  C  N  O  T  E  P  A  D
H  U  Y  U  V  L  O  M  D  A
Q  C  Z  S  P  K  G  H  L  I
```

This is another picture sudoku! Can you complete the grid below so there is just one left turn, one right turn, one up arrow, and one down arrow, in each row, each column, and inside each set of four boxes? Some of them have been filled in for you to make a start!

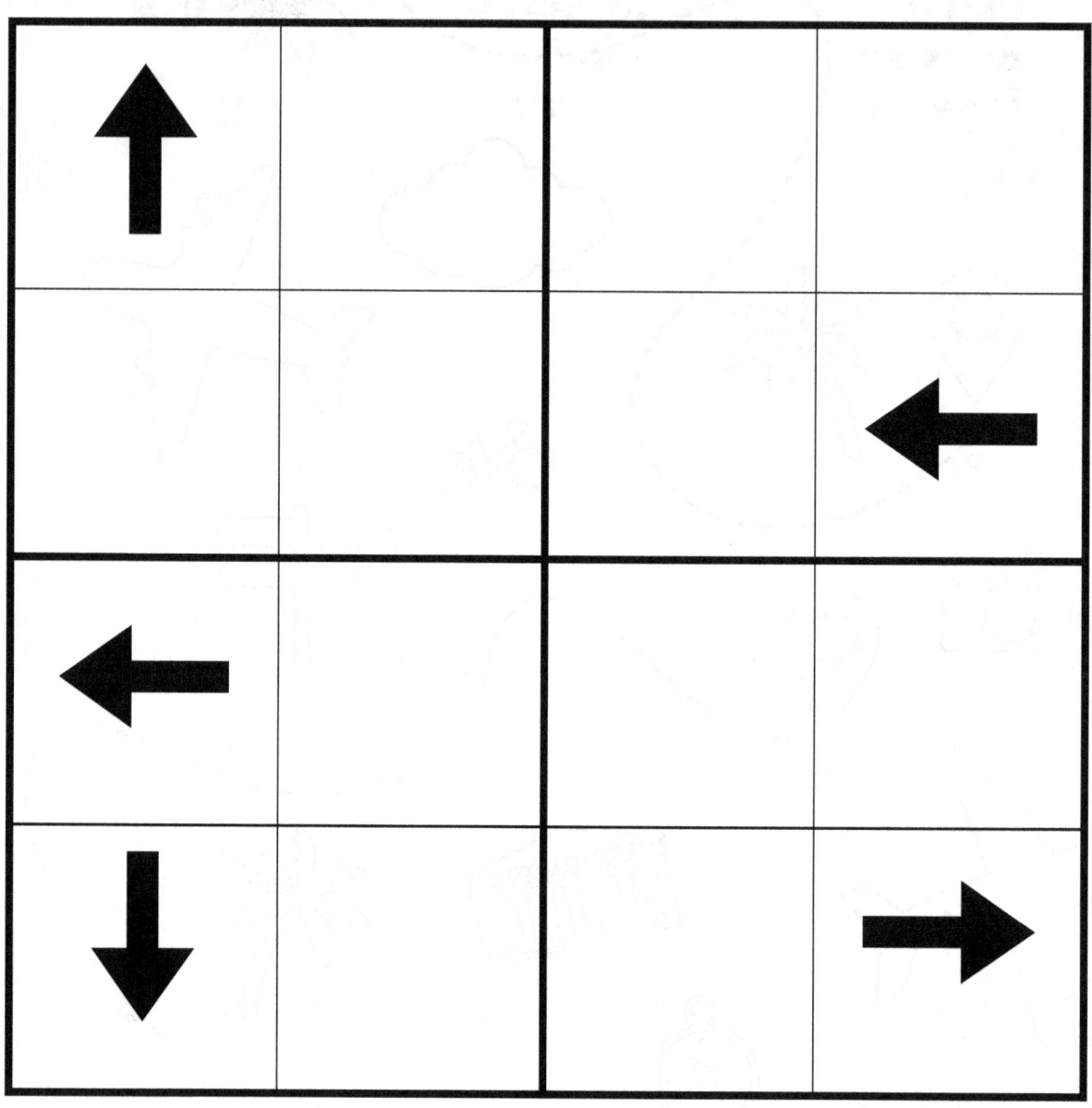

Can you spot five differences between these two road signs?

Match each speed sign on the left with the number exactly twice as fast on the right!

Fifteen of the letters in the grid below appear twice, while five of them only appear once. Reading from top to bottom, what do the five letters that only appear once spell out?

P	K	W	C	H	O	F
T	R	H	N	F	M	E
S	M	C	G	S	D	R
A	N	X	T	J	Q	K
J	Q	O	L	X	W	G

HIDDEN WORD: PEDAL

All the answers to these trivia questions begin with A. When you fit them into the grid, a word from your road trip will appear down the shaded column in the middle. What is the hidden word?

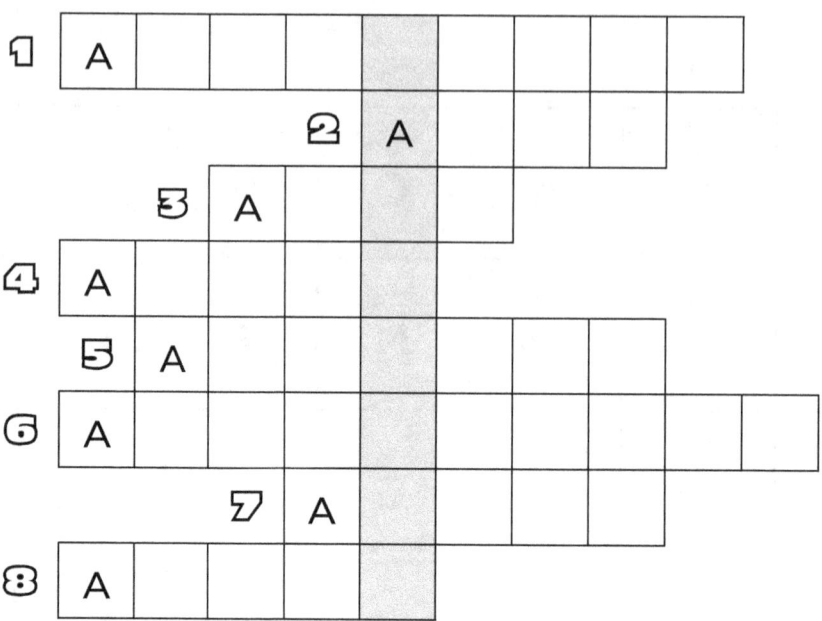

1 What was the surname of Neil, the first man on the Moon?

2 Who was Eve's husband in the Bible?

3 What is the world's largest continent?

4 The first of what month is known as "Fool's Day"?

5 What kind of building is Heathrow in London?

6 What is the person who manages an auction called?

7 What kind of fruit is a Granny Smith?

8 Which book character had an adventure in Wonderland?

Are there more traffic lights or pedestrian crossing lights on this page?

Can you solve these road sign sums?

1. 30 + 30 = _____

2. 50 − 20 = _____

3. 50 ÷ 10 = _____

4. 20 + 40 = _____

There are lots of different types of cars, of course! How many of these can you spot in the grid below?

- ☐ **COUPE**
- ☐ **ESTATE**
- ☐ **HATCHBACK**
- ☐ **JEEP**
- ☐ **MINI**
- ☐ **SALOON**
- ☐ **SEDAN**
- ☐ **SOFTTOP**
- ☐ **SUV**
- ☐ **TRUCK**

H	B	B	P	R	E	Z	G	C	Q
X	A	E	V	S	R	R	V	O	K
D	E	T	T	C	R	L	B	U	C
J	L	A	C	M	I	N	I	P	U
D	T	H	N	H	W	O	P	E	R
E	V	O	E	R	B	V	F	M	T
N	O	O	L	A	S	A	U	J	N
S	O	F	T	T	O	P	C	S	E
N	A	D	E	S	S	U	D	K	D
I	F	B	A	S	X	J	N	Z	J

Let's stop for a roadside picnic! Can you unjumble all the things below that you might have in your picnic basket?

1. **PALPE**   _ _ _ _ _

2. **RNAOGE**   O _ _ _ _ _

3. **NDASWHCI**   _ _ _ _ W _ _ H

4. **BNNAAA**   _ _ _ _ _ A

5. **KCAEPUC**   C _ P _ _ K _

6. **BLODIEGEG**   _ O _ _ I _ _ G G

52

Looks like the weather's changing! All the weather words below connect together in the grid. Can you figure out which word goes where?

- ☐ BLIZZARD
- ☐ CLOUDS
- ☐ DRIZZLE
- ☐ FOGGY
- ☐ FROST
- ☐ LIGHTNING
- ☐ RAIN
- ☐ SNOW
- ☐ STORM
- ☐ SUN
- ☐ THUNDER
- ☐ WIND

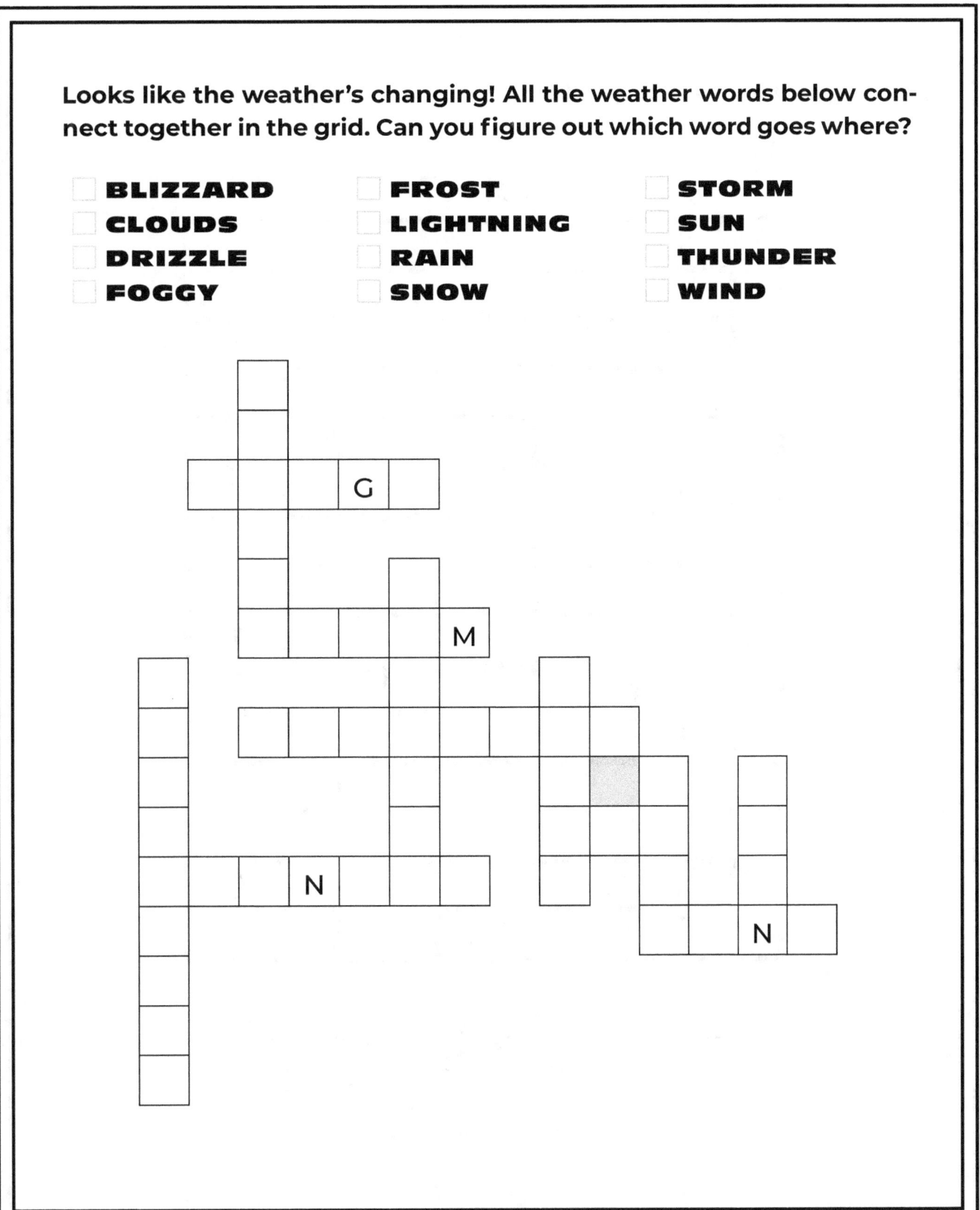

Let's go for a hike. Can you find your way to the hills?

Grab a pencil and let's make this road a little more interesting! Can you add a stop sign, some traffic lights, and three cars into this picture?

Let's get counting! Are there more left turns or right turns on this page?

56

Can you match the item on the left to the number that usually matches it on the right? The first answer has been written in for you to make a start!

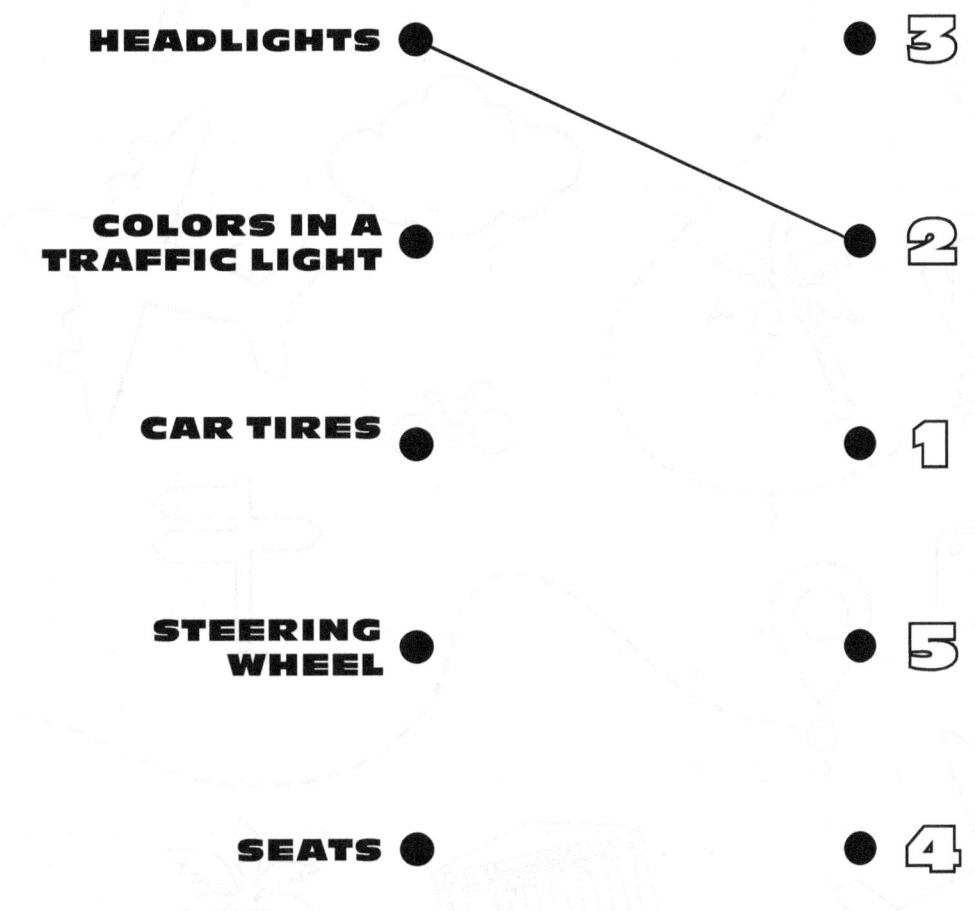

Here's a tricky wordsearch like no other! The word ROADTRIP is only written once in the grid below. It might be written in any direction—up or down, left or right, straight or diagonal, backwards or forwards. Can you spot it?

R	P	T	I	R	P	D	O	A
A	O	A	R	O	I	R	I	D
D	I	R	T	P	R	R	P	T
R	R	O	D	A	T	R	P	R
D	O	I	A	A	D	A	A	I
A	R	A	O	A	A	T	O	P
O	A	R	D	R	O	D	R	A
R	T	R	I	R	R	A	O	R

Here's another picture sudoku! Can you complete the grid below so there is just one pair of sunglasses, one beach flag, one sun, and one cloud, in each row, each column, and inside each set of four boxes? Some of them have been filled in for you to make a start!

Feeling a little thirsty? All the hot and cold drinks below connect together in the grid. Can you figure out where each word goes?

- COFFEE
- COLA
- HOT CHOCOLATE
- ICED TEA
- KOMBUCHA
- LEMONADE
- MILKSHAKE
- ORANGE JUICE
- SODA
- TEA
- TONIC
- WATER

Five taxi drivers—Sam, Sean, Simon, Sandra, and Stefano—each have a job in town at a different location: the station, the airport, the theatre, the hospital, and the mall. Based on the clues, can you figure out which driver is going where?

1 Sandra isn't going to the theatre or the mall

2 The driver going to the hospital has a name that ends in a vowel

3 Simon and Sean aren't going to the airport

4 The driver going to the theatre doesn't have an E in their name

5 The person with the longest name is going to the destination with the shortest name

SAM	
SEAN	
SIMON	
SANDRA	
STEFANO	

Let's make some trail mix to snack on in the car. How many of these ingredients can you find in the grid?

- ALMONDS
- CANDIES
- DRIED FRUIT
- GRAINS
- GRANOLA
- M AND MS
- PEANUTS
- PRETZELS
- RAISINS

```
J P L X S V S G S G
S M H I V T I H E R
S L A S U E N E I A
Q J E N N T D C D N
V E A Z D I C H N O
U E V Y T M S N A L
P J S Y N E S I C A
S N I A R G R N A C
A L M O N D S P P R
D R I E D F R U I T
```

Let's take a trip to the coast with these word jumbles. Can you unscramble these six things you might pack for a day at the beach?

1 TIEK   __ __ __ __

2 IIPCNC   __ __ C __ __ __

3 BCHLAEBAL   __ E __ C __ __ A __ __

4 RFEIBSE   __ R __ __ __ E __

5 SNCMAUER   __ U __ C __ __ __ M

6 LWOTE   __ __ __ __ __

Fifteen of the letters in the grid below appear twice, while five of them only appear once. Reading from top to bottom, what do the five letters that only appear once spell out?

B	F	U	A	P	D	G
X	R	T	O	M	H	C
P	Y	H	Y	I	F	T
K	U	G	C	V	X	S
E	O	K	A	S	B	M

HIDDEN WORD: DRIVE

Roads, streets, and avenues—they're not all the same! All the words below connect together in this grid. Can you work out which word goes where?

- ☐ AVENUE
- ☐ BOULEVARD
- ☐ CROSSING
- ☐ FREEWAY
- ☐ HIGHWAY
- ☐ LANE
- ☐ OVERPASS
- ☐ ROUTE
- ☐ SHORTCUT
- ☐ SIDE ROAD
- ☐ STREET
- ☐ THOROUGHFARE

Can you take the car to the campsite?

Can you solve these road sign sums?

1) 20 + 20 = _____

2) 50 − 10 = _____

3) 40 ÷ 20 = _____

4) 40 + 30 = _____

All the answers to these trivia questions begin with S. When you fit them into the grid, a word from your road trip will appear down the shaded column in the middle. What is the hidden word?

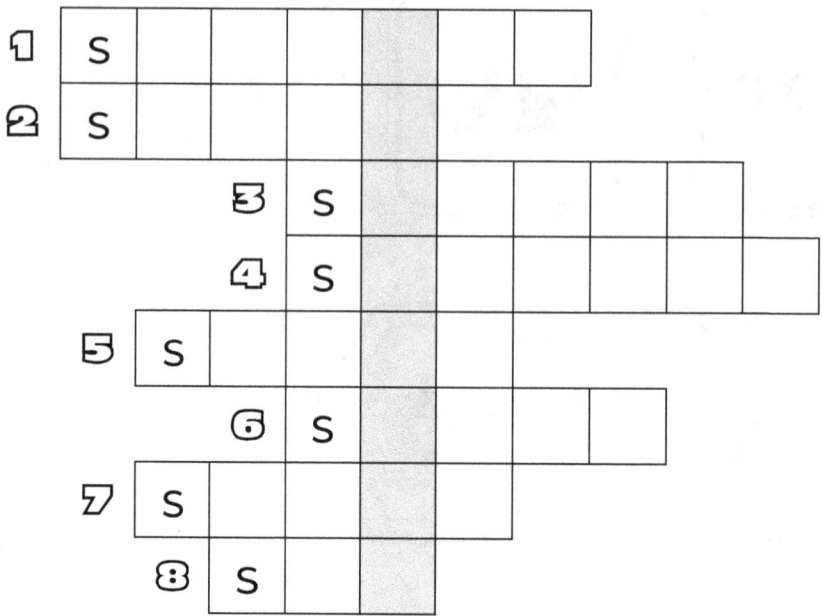

1 In what US city is the Space Needle?

2 Glucose is a natural form of what sweetener?

3 Which planet is famous for its rings?

4 On TV, what is Homer, Marge, Bart, and Lisa's surname?

5 In clothing sizes, what does S stand for?

6 What is the surname of the Oscar-winning actor Will, who starred in Independence Day and Aladdin?

7 In what country is the city of Madrid?

8 How many is half of a dozen?

Which of these road signs appears the most times in the grid below?

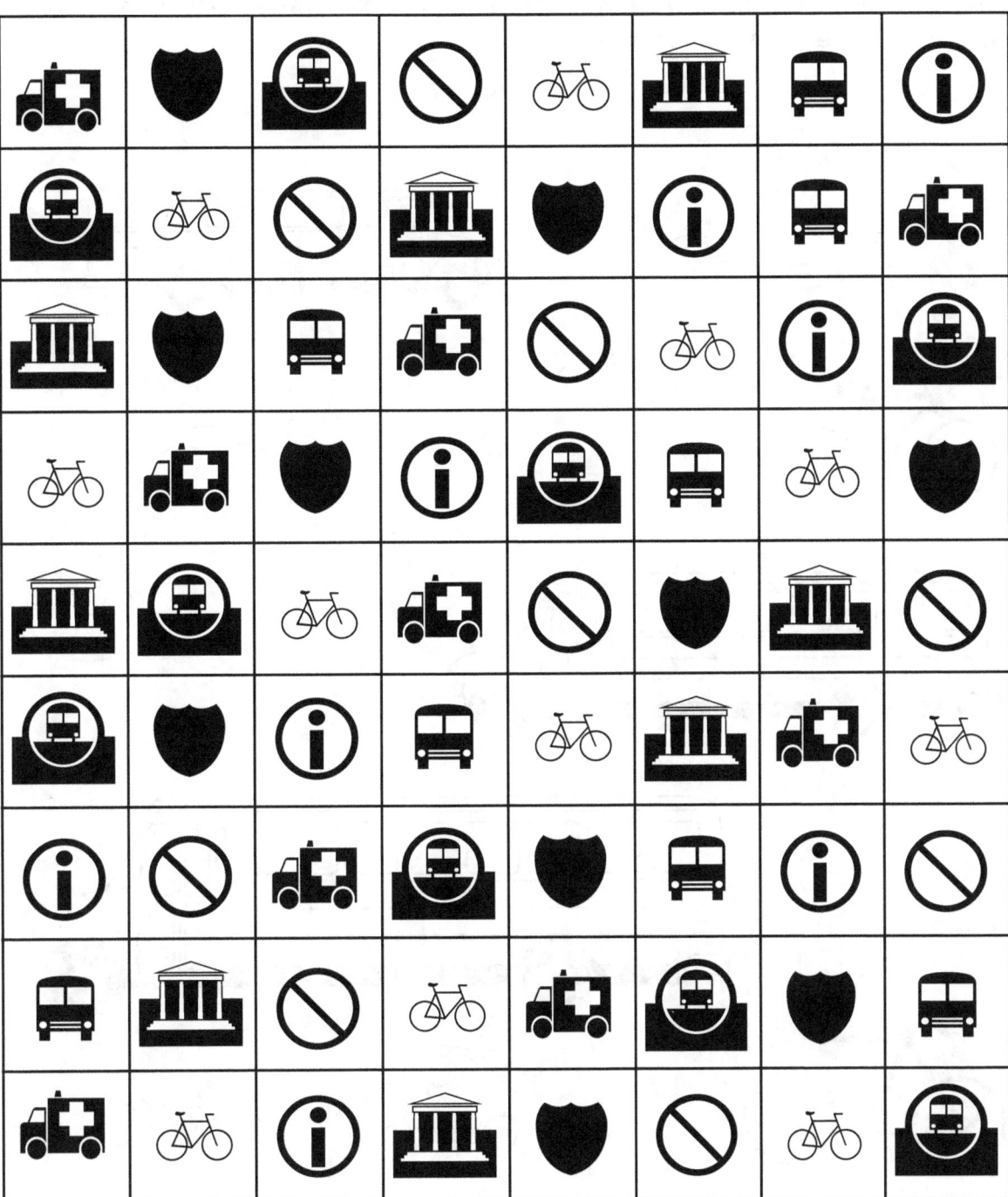

Let's see if you can work this out! There are three school buses, four cars, and three bicycles on this page. So how many wheels would all those vehicles have in total?

Keep your eyes on the sky for this next wordsearch! How many of these airborne things can you see?

- ☐ **AIRPLANE**
- ☐ **BALLOON**
- ☐ **BLIMP**
- ☐ **EAGLE**
- ☐ **HANG GLIDER**
- ☐ **HAWK**
- ☐ **PELICAN**
- ☐ **SEAGULL**
- ☐ **SWALLOW**

```
A E Y I G S C S K W
J I R F A F E W G O
N A R S C A A B O L
F O F P G H O L H L
Q E O U L O C I E A
J J L L F A T M A W
C L R U L J N P G S
P E L I C A N E L J
N L H Z C K B H E I
R E D I L G G N A H
```

And keep your eyes on the sky for this one too! The 12 birds listed below connect together in the grid. Can you figure out where each word goes?

- ☐ BLUEJAY
- ☐ TRAGOPAN
- ☐ EAGLE
- ☐ ROBIN
- ☐ FALCON
- ☐ FLAMINGO
- ☐ GOOSE
- ☐ GULL
- ☐ KESTREL
- ☐ PELICAN
- ☐ SWAN
- ☐ THRUSH
- ☐ VULTURE
- ☐ CROW
- ☐ PHEASANT

Five radio stations—WABC, WDEF, WGHI, WJKL, and WMNO—each play a different style of music: pop, rock, classical, jazz, and country. Based on the clues below, can you work out which station plays which genre?

1 WABC does not play classical or jazz

2 The station that plays pop doesn't have a vowel in its name

3 The country music station comes alphabetically after the pop station

4 The classical station has a name that ends in a vowel

5 WDEF doesn't play classical music

WABC	
WDEF	
WGHI	
WJKL	
WMNO	

Time for another picture sudoku! Can you complete the grid below so there is one 10, one 20, one 30, and one 40 speed limit sign in each row, each column, and inside each set of four boxes? Some of them have been filled in for you to make a start!

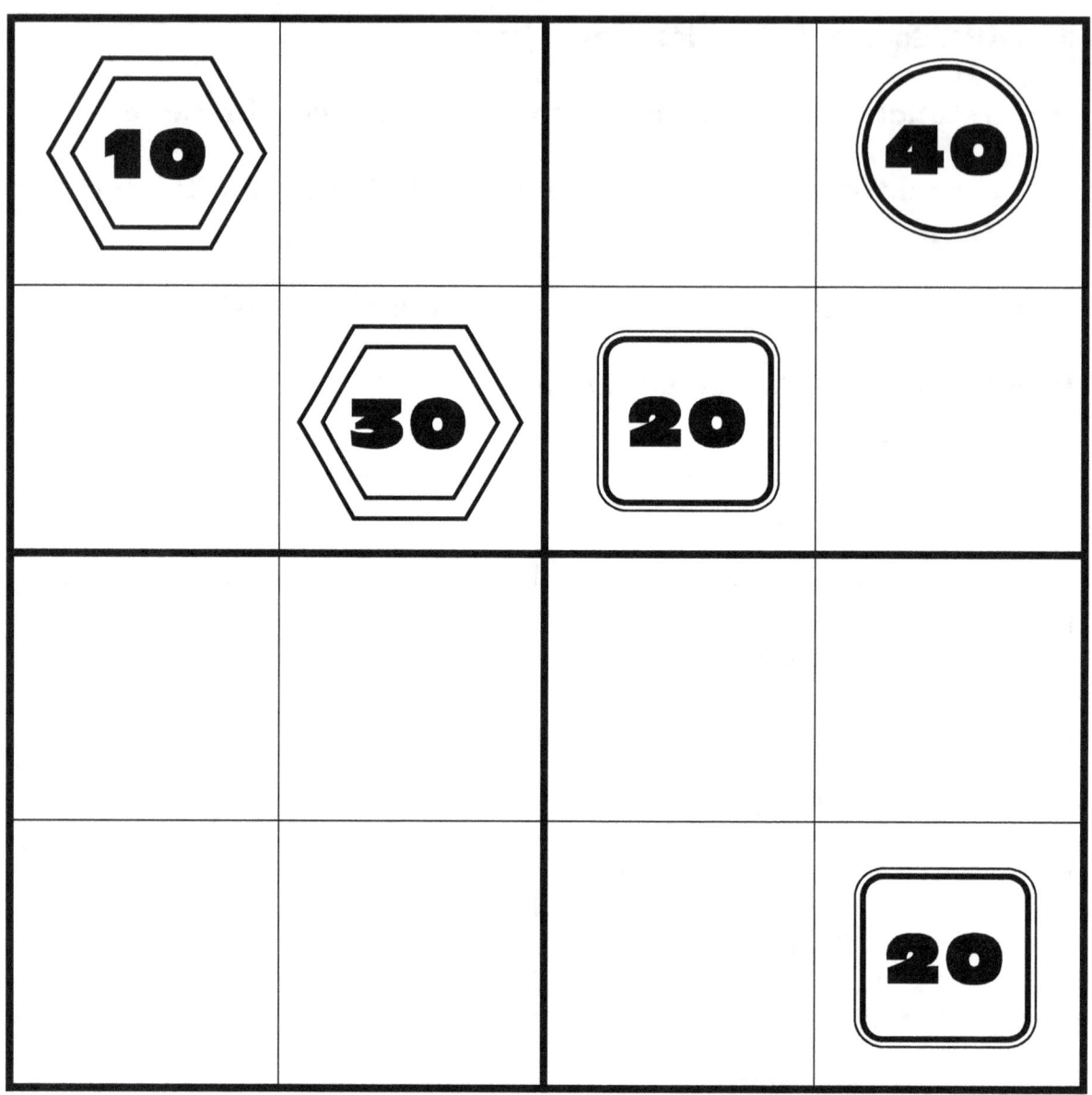

Uh oh... Looks like this journey's being held up! Can you unjumble these six things that might delay your trip?

1 TFIRFAC MAJ   _ A F _ _ C _ _ M

2 LTAF RIET   _ L T _ _ R _ _

3 TOPS INGS   S _ _ P _ _ G _

4 DOARRWSKRO   _ O _ _ W _ _ K _

5 DBA AETHRWE   _ _ _ W _ _ H _ _

6 CLSODE DOAR   C L _ _ _ _ _ A D

75

Can you take the car into the city?

76

Fifteen of the letters in the grid below appear twice, while five of them only appear once. Reading from top to bottom, what do the five letters that only appear once spell out?

Q	P	F	B	C	D	L
S	B	N	I	P	F	Z
Z	Q	G	V	J	S	M
E	D	E	X	H	R	M
N	J	X	C	T	V	R

HIDDEN WORD: LIGHT

Each of the road signs on this page has a pair—all, that is, except one! Match the pairs then draw the sign that doesn't have a pair to match with in the box at the bottom of the page.

The unmatched sign is:

The answers to these questions all begin with D. When you fit them into the grid, a word will appear down the shaded column in the middle. What is the word?

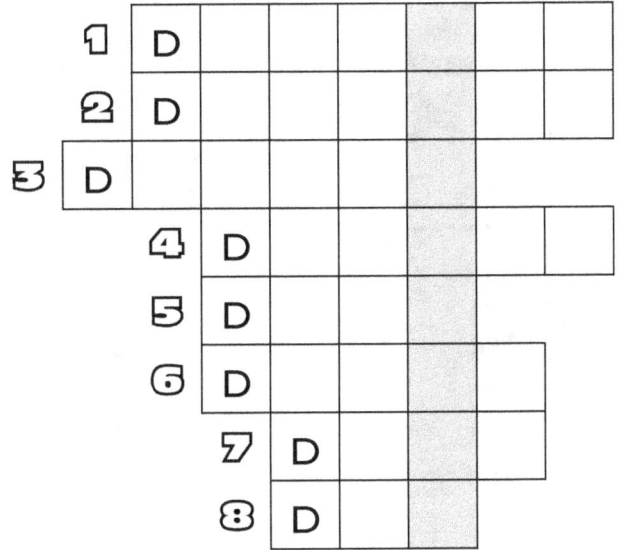

1 What is the name of the main character—played by Judy Garland in the famous film—in the Wizard of Oz?

2 What is the name of the famous vampire created by the author Bram Stoker?

3 What word is shortened to "Dr." before someone's name?

4 What movie studio made The Little Mermaid?

5 What word can mean a ball of water and to let go?

6 In the Bible, who killed the giant Goliath?

7 Whose wife would be called a "duchess"?

8 What is a female deer called?

Let's get counting! Are there more signs for the airport, or more signs for the bus station on this page?

How about some music? Turn on the radio and let's see how many of these music genres you can find in the wordsearch grid below.

- [ ] **BLUEGRASS**
- [ ] **CLASSICAL**
- [ ] **COUNTRY**
- [ ] **DANCE**
- [ ] **HIPHOP**
- [ ] **JAZZ**
- [ ] **LATIN**
- [ ] **POP**
- [ ] **ROCK N ROLL**

V	V	A	U	C	C	E	P	C	Q
C	H	I	P	H	O	P	O	B	Z
L	K	W	E	W	L	U	P	Z	E
A	A	M	N	R	N	M	A	Q	C
S	M	D	N	T	D	J	L	R	N
S	S	A	R	G	E	U	L	B	A
I	U	Y	N	I	T	A	L	S	D
C	R	O	C	K	N	R	O	L	L
A	T	W	D	J	V	E	A	J	Q
L	U	Z	O	P	B	Z	K	S	B

Five road junctions—61, 62, 63, 64, and 65—lead to five different towns: Metropolis, Homeville, Cityburg, Townfield, and Hamleton. Based on the clues below, can you work out which junction leads to which town?

1 You reach Metropolis by taking a junction that is an even number

2 To get to Homeville, you need to take the junction before Metropolis

3 Junction 63 leads to somewhere with an 8-letter name

4 Junction 65 does not lead to Cityburg

5 Junction 64 leads to somewhere beginning with H

61	
62	
63	
64	
65	

Fifteen of the letters in the grid below appear twice, while five of them only appear once. Reading from top to bottom, what do the five letters that only appear once spell out?

T	A	Z	B	X	C	G
M	W	H	I	M	K	F
P	P	R	V	G	O	O
K	C	H	Y	A	Z	E
B	X	S	Y	W	F	V

HIDDEN WORD: TIRES

Let's turn the radio on and listen in for this one! All these words connect together in the grid. Can you figure out where each word goes?

- [ ] **CHARTS**
- [ ] **CHAT**
- [ ] **CONTESTS**
- [ ] **INTERVIEWS**
- [ ] **LIVE**
- [ ] **NEWS**
- [ ] **PHONE-INS**
- [ ] **POP MUSIC**
- [ ] **PRESENTERS**
- [ ] **SONGS**
- [ ] **SPORT**
- [ ] **STATION**
- [ ] **TRAFFIC**
- [ ] **UPDATES**
- [ ] **WEATHER REPORT**

Can you solve this final set of road sign sums?

1) 10 + 50 = _____

2) 30 − 20 = _____

3) 30 ÷ 10 = _____

4) 50 + 50 = _____

Here's another picture sudoku! Can you complete the grid below so there is one 12 o'clock, one 3 o'clock, one 6 o'clock, and one 9 o'clock in each row, each column, and inside each set of four boxes? Some of them have been filled in for you to make a start!

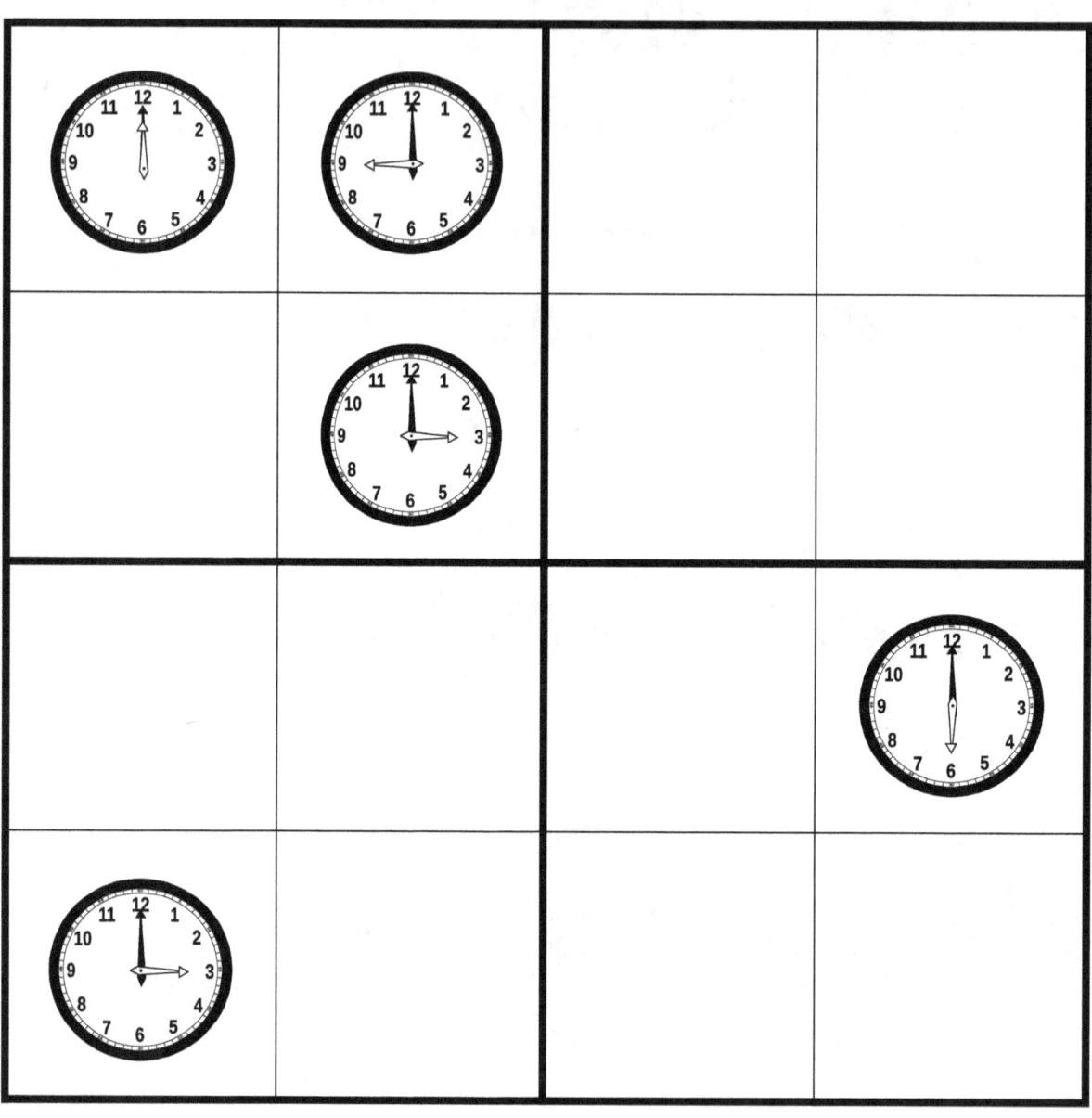

The answers to these questions all begin with S. When you fit them into the grid, a word will appear down the shaded column in the middle. What is the word?

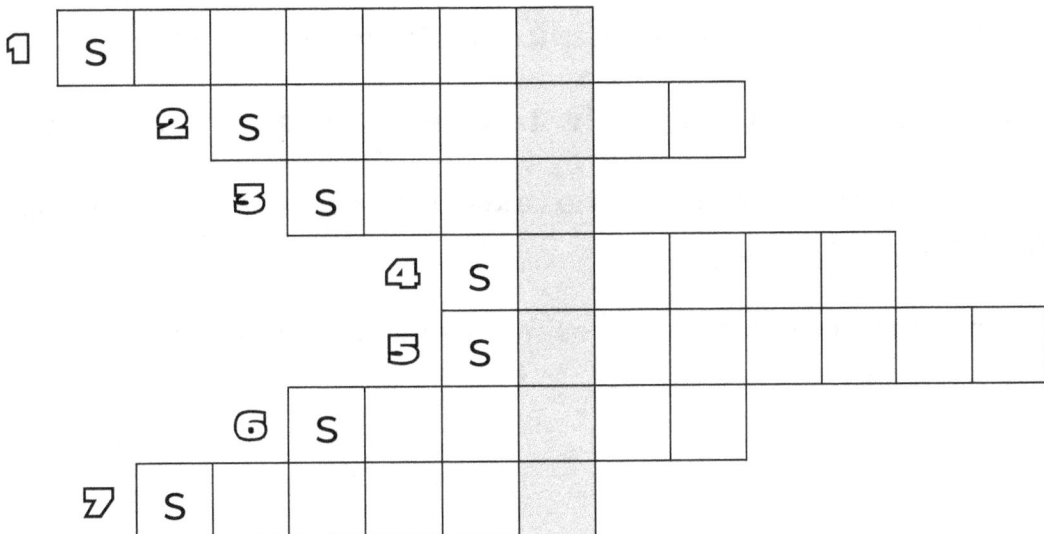

1 What food gives Popeye his strength?

2 What language is spoken in Mexico, Argentina, and Peru?

3 What is a male deer called?

4 What is the area of darkness cast behind an object by the sun or another source of light called?

5 In what sport did Michael Phelps become a famous Olympic champion?

6 What shape has four sides of equal length?

7 On what day of the week is Easter Day always celebrated?

Five mechanics—Bob, Charles, Donna, Eddie, and Felicity—are each working on five different vehicles: a truck, a taxi, a convertible, a sports car, and a motorbike. Based on the clues below, can you figure out who's working on what?

1 Neither of the female mechanics work on motorbikes

2 The mechanic working on the truck also has a 5-letter name

3 The mechanic working on the taxi doesn't have any of the letters in TAXI in their name!

4 The mechanic with the longest name is working on the vehicle with the longest name!

BOB	
CHARLES	
DONNA	
EDDIE	
FELICITY	

If you're on a long trip, you might have to strap some things to the roof of your car! How many of these roof rack items can you unjumble below?

1 BECYICL   _ _ _ I _ Y _ _ _

2 SFRUBORAD   _ U _ _ B _ _ _ D

3 NTET   _ _ _ _

4 FLOG BLCUS   G _ _ _ _ _ _ _ B S

5 PARES RITE   _ P _ _ _ _ _ _ E

6 LGGGUEA   _ _ G _ _ G _

Don't forget your suitcase! How many of these bags and holdalls can you find in the grid below?

- ☐ **BACKPACK**
- ☐ **CLUTCH**
- ☐ **DUFFEL**
- ☐ **HANDBAG**
- ☐ **RUCKSACK**
- ☐ **SATCHEL**
- ☐ **SUITCASE**
- ☐ **TOTE BAG**
- ☐ **VALISE**

```
B R Q G F R Y C Q X
L A O X C U U J T D
E C C N V C X G D S
H G L K C K D K U W
C A G U P S M I F E
T B A F T A T T F V
A E H R U C C J E I
S T J I A K H K L U
H O Q S E S I L A V
T T E H A N D B A G
```

Uh oh, we need to swing by the garage for some repairs! Can you guide the car there?

All these road sign names connect together in the grid. Can you figure out where each one goes?

- CYCLE
- DEAD END
- DETOUR
- EXIT
- HAZARD
- INTERSTATE
- LEFT TURN
- NO ENTRY
- PARKING
- RIGHT TURN
- SCENIC AREA
- SHOULDER WORK
- SPEED
- STOP
- YIELD

Can you match each of these car parts to the number its pointing at in the picture? The first answer has been filled in for you to make a start!

- [ ] HUBCAP
- [ ] WING MIRROR
- [x] HEADLIGHT
- [ ] DOOR PANEL
- [ ] TIRE
- [ ] TRUNK
- [ ] WINDSHIELD
- [ ] BUMPER

1 Headlight
2 _____
3 _____
4 _____
5 _____
6 _____
7 _____
8 _____

Careful you don't get lost! How many of the words to do with maps, atlases, and road map symbols can you find in the grid below?

- ARROW
- BORDER
- COMPASS
- COORDINATE
- GRIDLINES
- HIGHWAY
- INDEX
- NAVIGATE
- PAGES

```
I  J  T  R  W  U  T  O  G  N
W  N  O  O  S  E  G  A  P  A
N  A  R  B  O  R  D  E  R  V
D  R  C  O  M  P  A  S  S  I
A  D  A  Z  D  P  R  X  V  G
G  R  I  D  L  I  N  E  S  A
Y  A  W  H  G  I  H  D  F  T
D  J  G  Q  A  J  X  N  N  E
P  S  O  Y  T  K  Q  I  X  I
E  T  A  N  I  D  R  O  O  C
```

Fifteen of the letters in the grid below appear twice, while five of them only appear once. Reading from top to bottom, what do the five letters that only appear once spell out?

G	A	M	C	B	Q	F
W	K	W	O	U	H	N
S	R	F	T	U	A	D
S	K	B	P	N	G	E
L	R	P	H	D	Q	C

HIDDEN WORD: M O T E L

Pencils at the ready again! Draw one person in the first car, two people in the second car, three people in the third, and four people in the fourth!

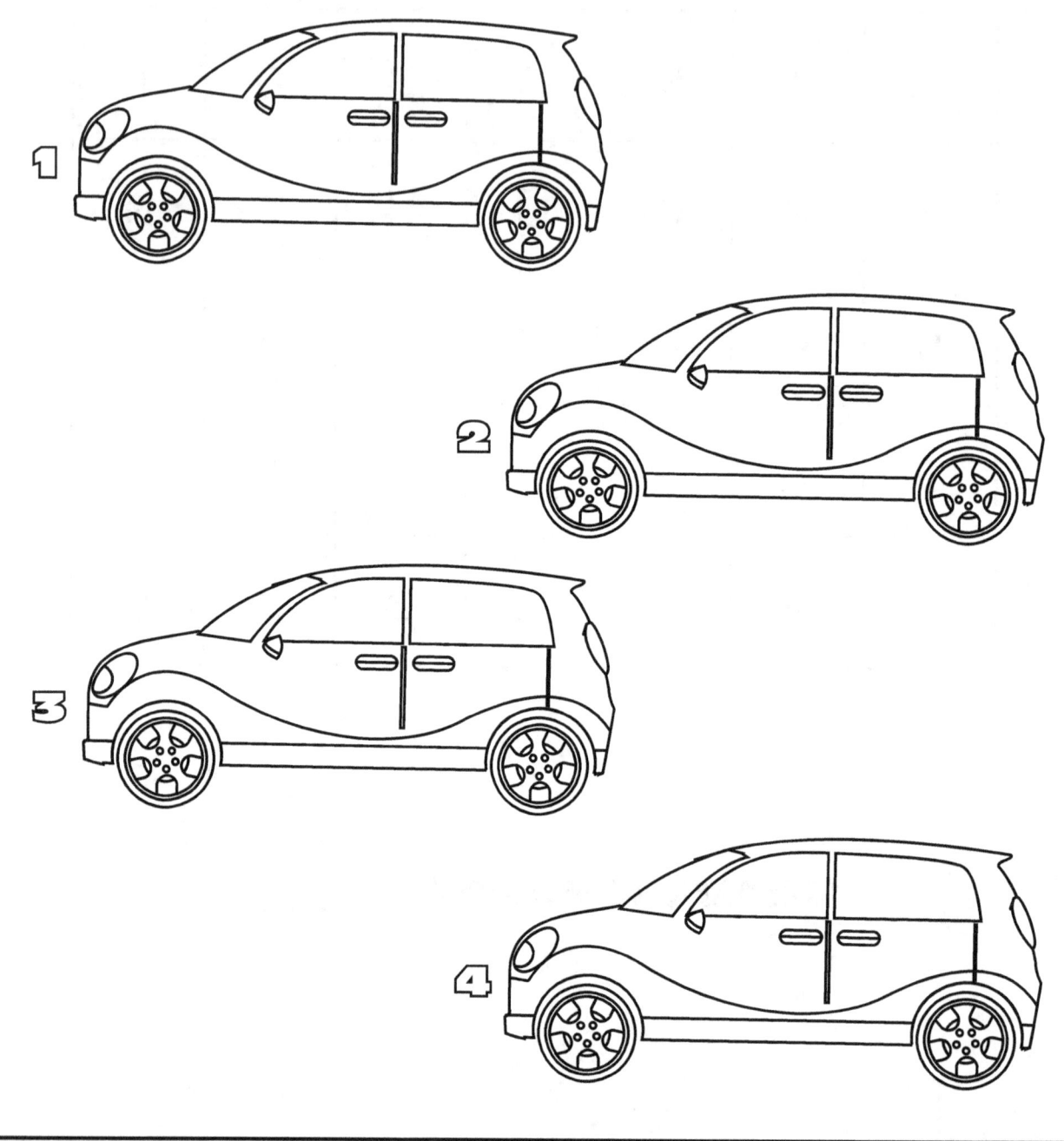

The answers to these questions all begin with C. When you fit them into the grid, a word will appear down the shaded column in the middle. What is the word?

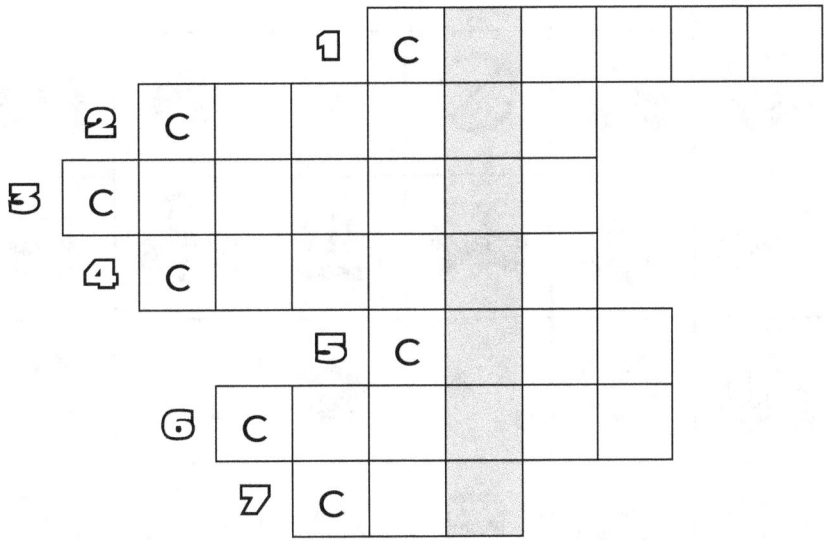

1 Ottawa is the capital city of what North American country?

2 What kind of food is mozzarella?

3 In Greek mythology, what kind of monster was a giant that had only one eye in the middle of its forehead?

4 What is the past tense of the verb to catch?

5 What is the French word for coffee, which is used in English as the name of a small restaurant or coffee shop?

6 What is the stiffened neckline of a shirt called?

7 What kind of animal is a Siamese?

Which of these road signs appears the most times in the grid below?

We're almost there! How many of these things you'll find at the hotel when you arrive can you unscramble?

1 MYG   _ _ _

2 SMWINMIG LOPO   _ _ I M _ _ _ _ O O _

3 CKHEC-NI   _ H E _ _ - _ N

4 PKARNGI TOL   _ _ _ K _ _ G _ _ T

5 RSTAURNETA   _ E _ T _ _ R _ _ T

6 MORO VERCIES   _ _ _ M _ S E _ V _ _ _

Here's another picture sudoku! Can you complete the grid below so there is one 12 o'clock, one 3 o'clock, one 6 o'clock, and one 9 o'clock in each row, each column, and inside each set of four boxes? Some of them have been filled in for you to make a start!

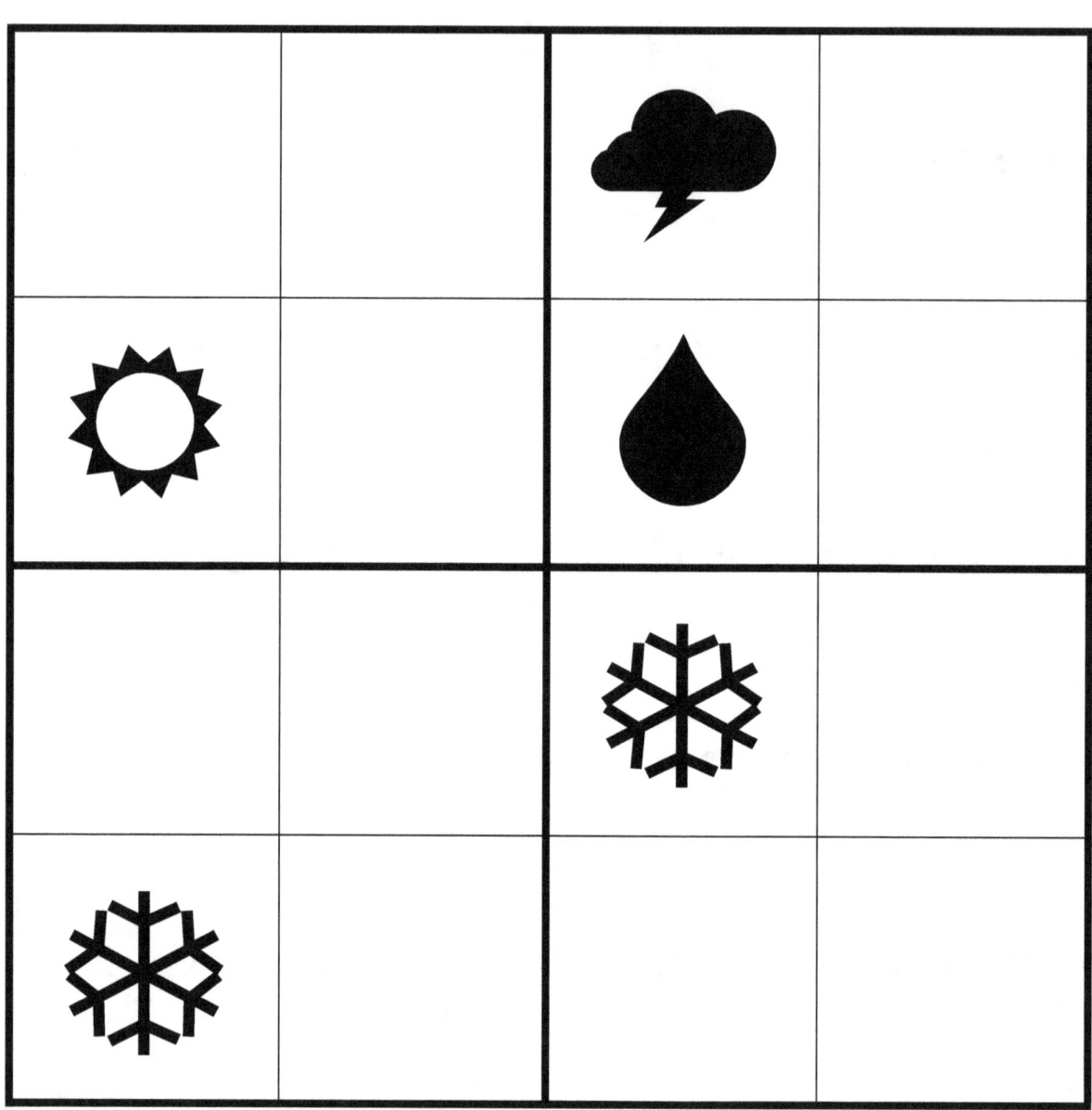

There are a lot of things that go into a car besides just the people! All these car parts and driving additions connect together in the grid below. Can you figure out where each word goes?

- [ ] **AIR FRESHENER**
- [ ] **ANTIFREEZE**
- [ ] **CLEANER**
- [ ] **COOLANT**
- [ ] **DIESEL**
- [ ] **DUSTER**
- [ ] **GASOLINE**
- [ ] **OIL**
- [ ] **SCREEN WASH**
- [ ] **SEALANT**
- [ ] **SPARE TIRE**
- [ ] **WATER**

One last pitstop before we arrive. How many of these items and souvenirs can you pick up from the roadside store?

- ☐ **BUMPER / STICKER**
- ☐ **CANDIES**
- ☐ **CHEWING GUM**
- ☐ **KEYRING**
- ☐ **POSTER**
- ☐ **ROADMAP**
- ☐ **SUNHAT**

```
G C N R O A D M A P
N H L A M Y Q W M X
I E B T A H N U S C
R W S U L E W G A V
Y I T T M B Y N I R
E N I R V P D F E Z
K G C B I I E T L B
C G K H E H S R L N
E U E S Z O S P B V
P M R C P V C T C D
```

We're almost at the end of our journey! Can you guide the car home?

There are five people in the car: a mom, a dad, a grandad, a son, and a daughter. Each person is doing something: driving, navigating, reading, eating, and sleeping. Based on the clues below, can you work out who is doing what?

1 The daughter isn't driving

2 The person who's eating and the person who's sleeping are both male

3 The driver is female

4 The oldest person is holding a map

5 The son isn't sleeping

MOM	
DAD	
GRANDAD	
SON	
DAUGHTER	

CONCLUSION

And with that last logic puzzle, we've arrived at our destination! Time to park up, put away your pens and pencils, and stretch your legs after a long journey.

We very much hope you've enjoyed your Road Trip Activity Book! And if you've worked through all 100 puzzles, games, and activities here, we hope that you've thoroughly taxed your brain—and maybe learned a little something along the way too!

If you've not quite managed all 100 games, though, don't worry. There will always be plenty to keep you busy on the return journey!

SOLUTIONS

107

5

7

There are 12 ambulances 🚑 in the grid, more than any other symbol!

8

1 Radio 2 Window 3 Driver 4 Pedal 5 Handbrake 6 Headrest

10

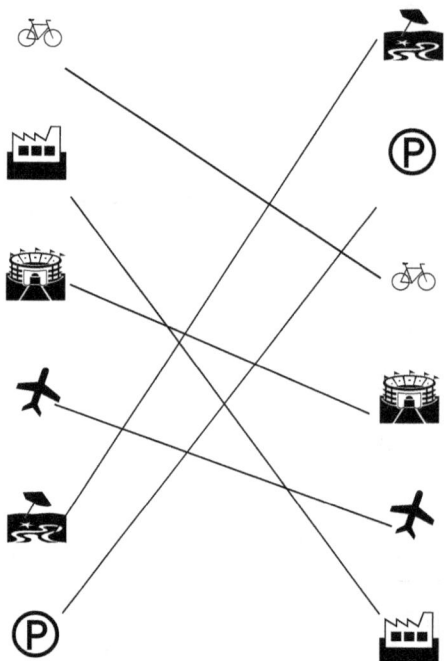

6

11

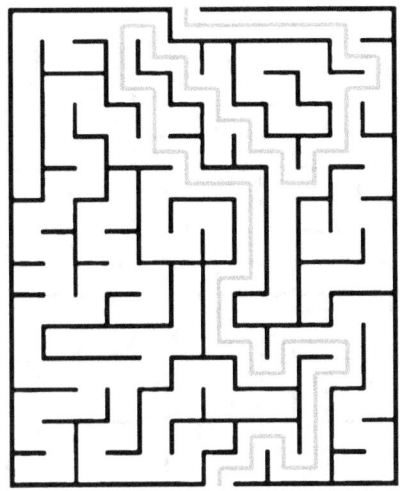

13

1 Truck 2 Jeep 3 Taxi 4 Pickup 5 Motorbike 6 Ambulance

14

Left. There are 15 left turns, but only 11 right turns!

15

S	T	S	A	Q	B	G	B	L	T
U	N	R	I	F	Y	A	C	A	U
N	E	E	R	D	G	E	X	B	X
H	A	G	P	S	C	I	N	J	V
A	V	N	L	C	I	R	A	O	Z
T	Z	E	A	D	M	C	P	T	M
P	U	S	N	C	K	M	V	Y	T
X	K	S	E	G	A	G	G	U	L
Q	B	A	S	T	E	K	C	I	T
C	U	P	A	S	S	P	O	R	T

12

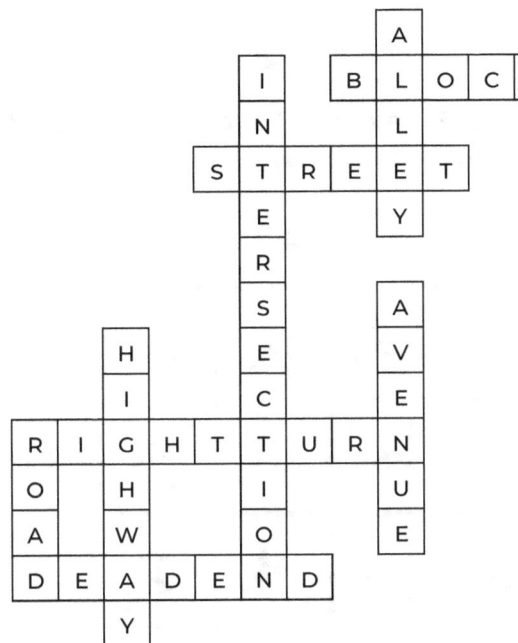

16

1. 20 2. 70 3. 3 4. 100

17

1 Paris 2 Piano 3 Panda 4 Pearl 5 Pillow 6 Pasta 7 Purple 8 Puck

The hidden word is SIDEWALK

18

The end of your trip = Destination

It keeps you safe! = Seatbelt

Where you might keep your bags = Trunk

Glass front of a vehicle = Windshield

It keeps you entertained with music = Radio

X-shaped road junction = crossroads

19

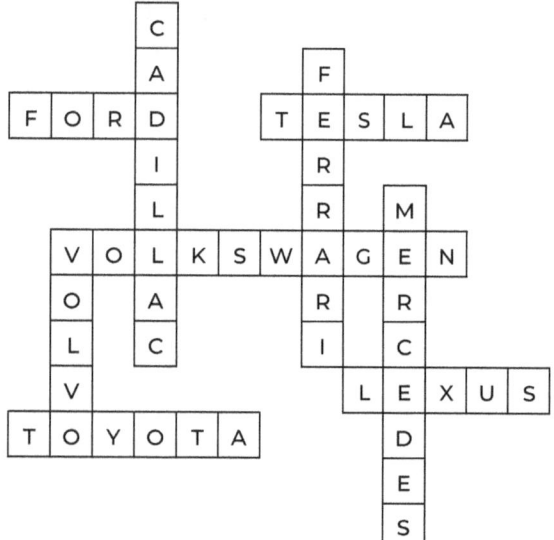

20

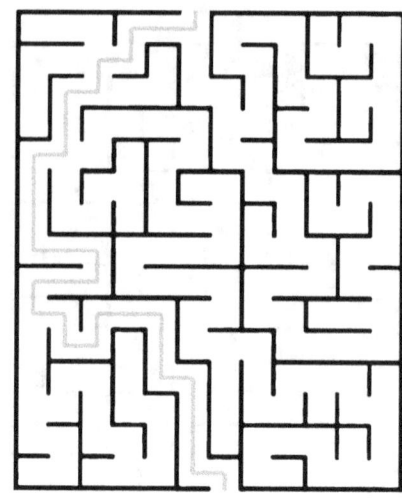

21

The hidden word is TRAIL.

22

1 Hills 2 Lakes 3 Forests 4 Parks 5 Motels 6 Mountains

24

25

30

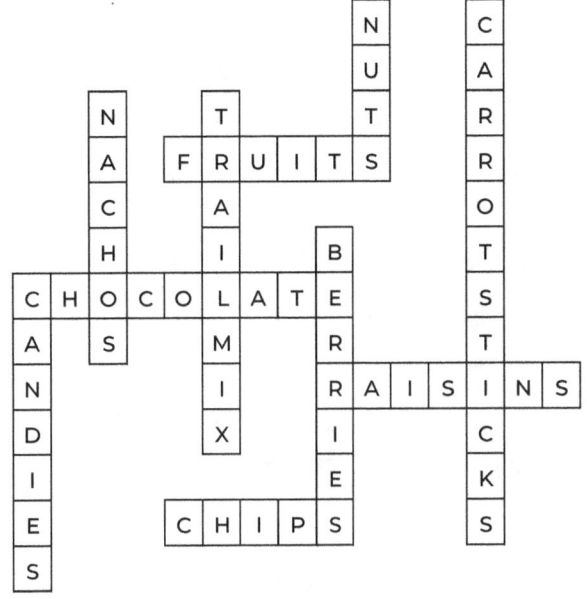

27

Stop signs. There are 12 Dead End signs, but 14 Stop signs.

28

1 Weeks 2 Walrus 3 Washington 4 Wrist 5 Wick 6 Water 7 West 8 White

The hidden word reading down the middle column is SUITCASE.

29

1 Sunglasses 2 Passport 3 Suitcase 4 Shorts 5 Hat 6 Sunscreen

31

1. 10 2. 50 3. 70 4. 4

32

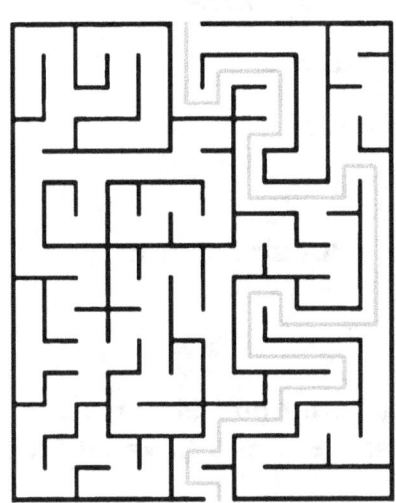

33

34

The letters that only appear once spell out GEARS.

35

Amanda = Airplane

Bruno = Bicycle

Carlo = Boat

Daniel = Car

Emily = Hot air balloon

37

1 Solar 2 Salmon 3 Signature 4 Sound 5 Sister 6 States 7 Seven 8 Sugar

The hidden word is ROADSTER

38

1 Tent 2 Bag 3 Blanket 4 Torch 5 Stove 6 Matches

39

Ambulances. There are 14 ambulances, but only 11 fire trucks.

40

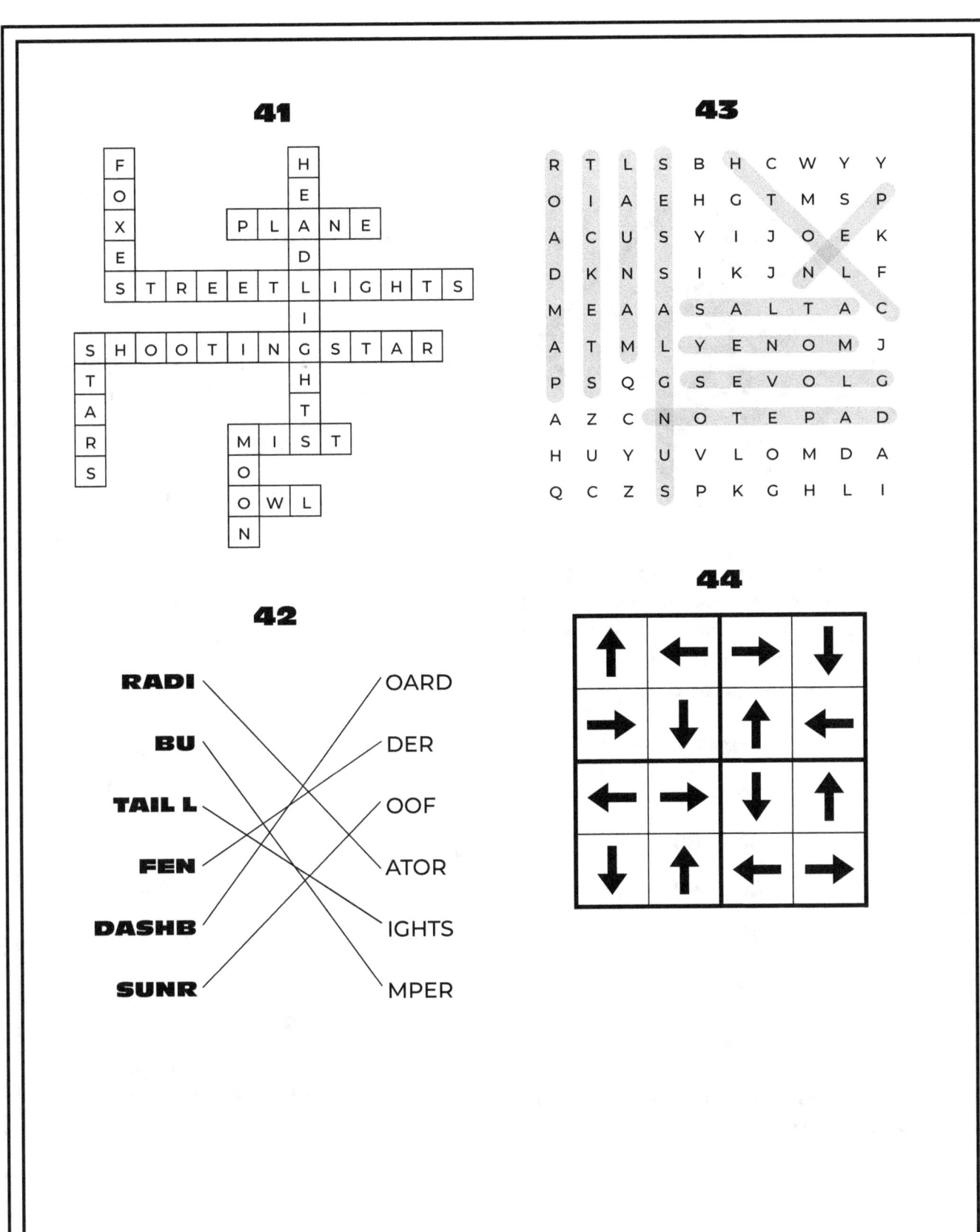

45

The figure is (1) wearing a hat and (2) a belt in the second picture; (3) the right arm is shorter; (4) the top horizontal line is shorter; and (5) the figure's left leg is longer.

46

10 — 20
40 — 80
20 — 40
15 — 30
30 — 60

47

The letters that only appear once spell PEDAL.

48

1 Armstrong 2 Adam 3 Asia 4 April 5 Airport 6 Auctioneer 7 Apple 8 Alice

The hidden word is TAILPIPE.

49

Traffic lights. There are 9 traffic lights, but only 8 pedestrian crossing signs.

50

1. 60 2. 30 3. 5 4. 60

51

H	B	B	P	R	E	Z	G	C	Q
X	A	E	V	S	R	R	V	O	K
D	E	T	T	C	R	L	B	U	C
J	L	A	C	M	I	N	I	P	U
D	T	H	N	H	W	O	P	E	R
E	V	O	E	R	B	V	F	M	T
N	O	O	L	A	S	A	U	J	N
S	O	F	T	T	O	P	C	S	E
N	A	D	E	S	S	U	D	K	D
I	F	B	A	S	X	J	N	Z	J

52

1 Apple 2 Orange 3 Sandwich 4 Banana 5 Cupcake 6 Boiled egg

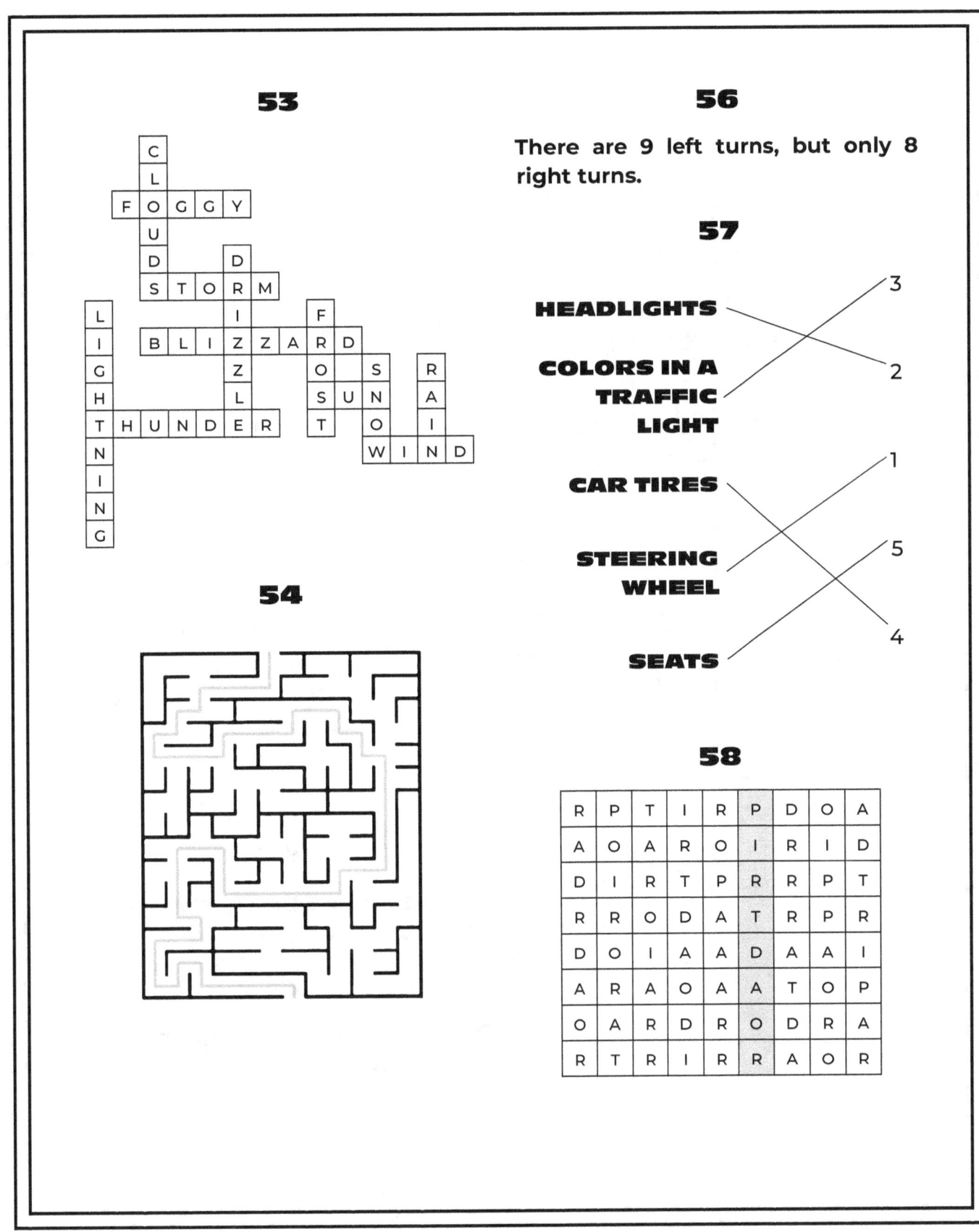

59

61

Sam = Airport

Sean = Station

Simon = Theatre

Sandra = Hospital

Stefano = Mall

60

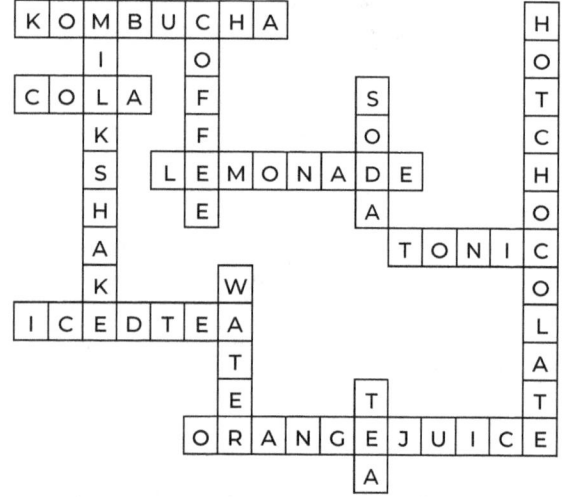

62

```
J P L X S V S G S G
S M H I V T I H E R
S L A S U E N E I A
Q J E N N T D C D N
V E A Z D I C H N O
U E V Y T M S N A L
P J S Y N E S I C A
S N I A R G R N A C
A L M O N D S P P R
D R I E D F R U I T
```

63

1 Kite 2 Picnic 3 Beachball 4 Frisbee 5 Sun cream 6 Tower

64

The letters that only appear once spell DRIVE.

65

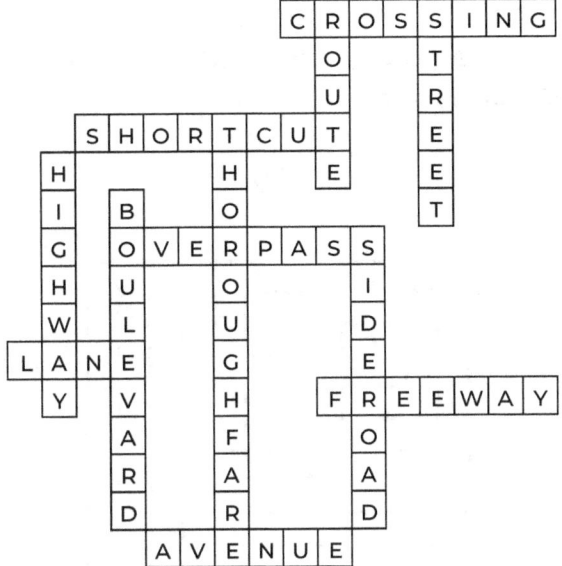

66

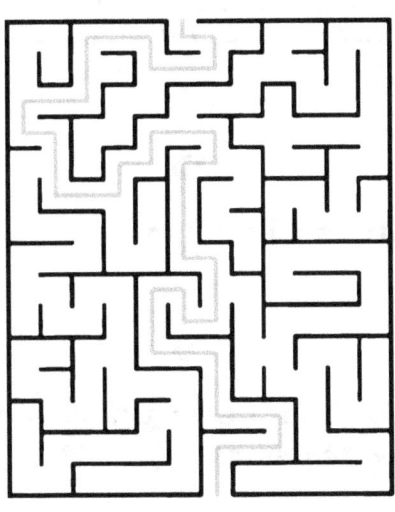

67

1. 40 2. 40 3. 2 4. 70

68

1 Seattle 2 Sugar 3 Saturn 4 Simpson 5 Small 6 Smith 7 Spain 8 Six.

The hidden answer is TRAIL MIX.

69

There are 11 bicycles, more than any other!

70

34. The three buses would have 12, the four cars would have 16, and the three bicycles would have 6.

71

72

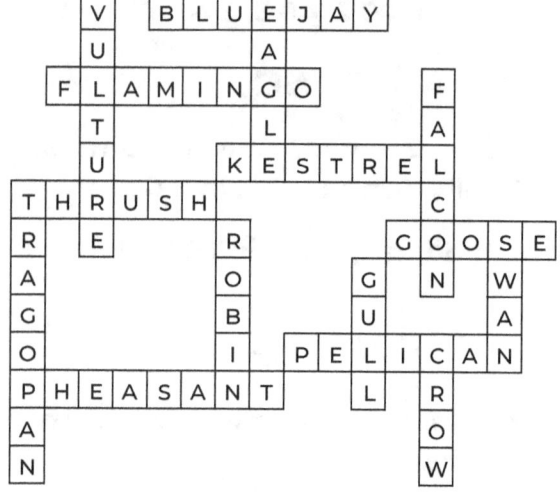

73

WABC = rock

WDEF = jazz

WGHI = classical

WJKL = pop

WMNO = country

74

10	20	30	40
40	30	20	10
20	40	10	30
30	10	40	20

75

1 Traffic jam 2 Flat tire 3 Stop sign 4 Roadworks 5 Bad weather 6 Closed road

76

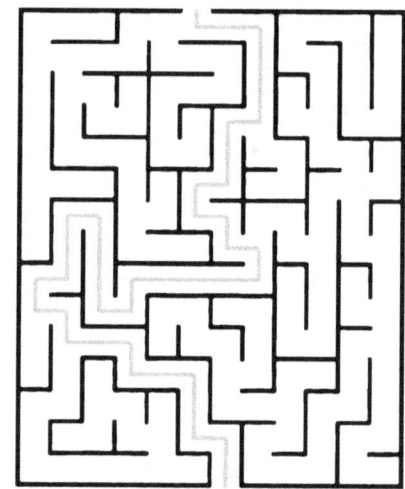

77

The letters used only once spell LIGHT.

78

The sign that doesn't have a match is the ambulance.

79

1 Dorothy 2 Dracula 3 Doctor 4 Disney 5 Drop 6 David 7 Duke 8 Doe

The hidden word is TURNPIKE.

80

There are 7 signs for the airport, but only 6 signs for the bus station.

81

82

61 = Homeville

62 = Metropolis

63 = Cityburg

64 = Hamleton

65 = Townfield

83

The letters used only once spell TIRES.

84

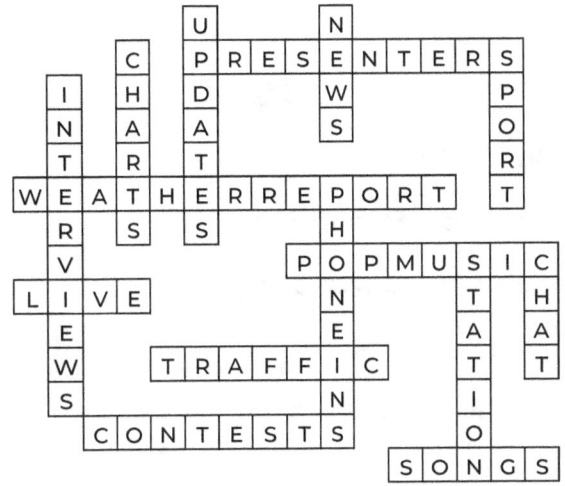

85

1. 60 2. 10 3. 3 4. 100

86

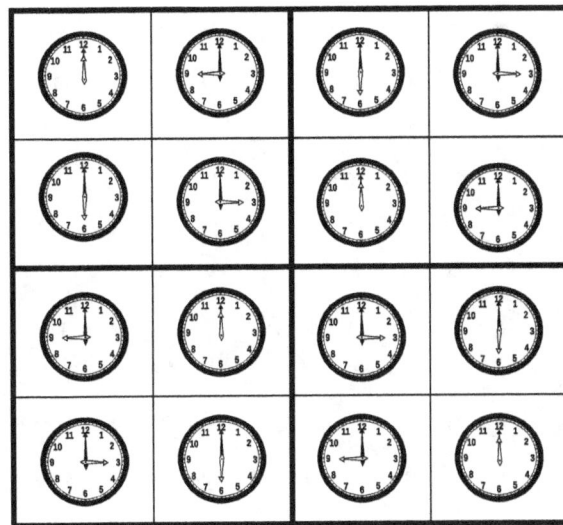

87

1 Spinach 2 Spanish 3 Stag 4 Shadow 5 Swimming 6 Square 7 Sunday

The hidden word is HIGHWAY.

88

Bob = Taxi

Charles = Motorbike

Donna = Sports Car

Eddie = Truck

Felicity = Convertible

89

1 Bicycle 2 Surfboard 3 Tent 4 Golf clubs 5 Spare tire 6 Luggage

90

91

92

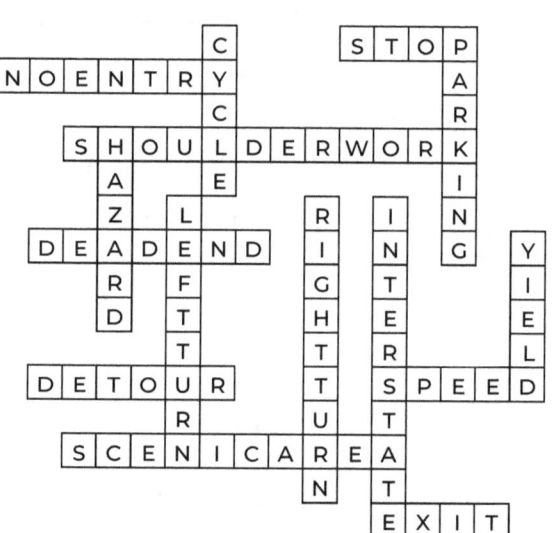

93

1 Headlight 2 Windshield 3 Door panel 4 Trunk 5 Hubcap 6 Wing mirror 7 Tire 8 Bumper

94

95

The letters used only once spell out MOTEL.

97

1 Canada 2 Cheese 3 Cyclops 4 Caught 5 Café 6 Collar 7 Cat

The hidden word is ASPHALT.

98

There are 12 No Entry signs 🚫.

99

1 Gym 2 Swimming pool 3 Check-in 4 Parking lot 5 Restaurant 6 Room service

100

101

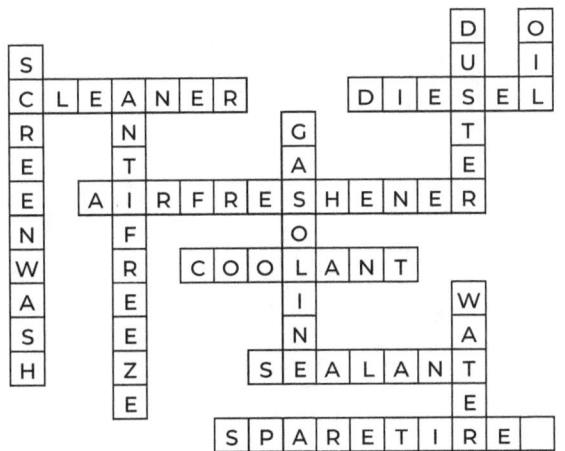

102

```
G C N R O A D M A P
N H L A M Y Q W M X
I E B T A H N U S C
R W S U L E W G A V
Y I T M B Y N I R
E N I R V P D F E Z
K G C B I I E T L B
C G K H E H S R L N
E U E S Z O S P B V
P M R C P V C T C D
```

103

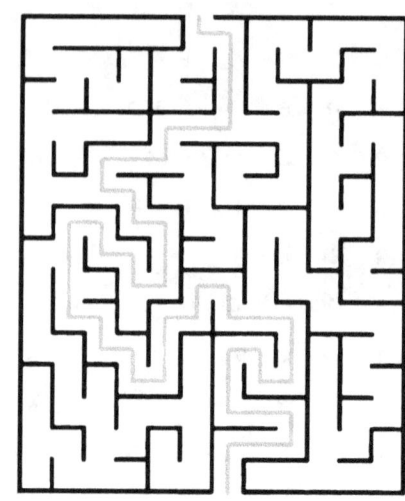

104

Mom = Driving

Dad = Sleeping

Grandad = Navigating

Son = Eating

Daughter = Reading

www.ingramcontent.com/pod-product-compliance
Lightning Source LLC
Chambersburg PA
CBHW081401070526
44583CB00020B/2630